FLATBREADS
FROM AROUND THE WORLD

Donna Rathmell German

BRISTOL PUBLISHING ENTERPRISES, INC.
San Leandro, California

A NITTY GRITTY® COOKBOOK

Printed in the United States of America.

ISBN 1-55867-097-1

Cover design: Frank Paredes
Front cover photography: John Benson
Food stylist: Suzanne Carreiro

CONTENTS

*Thanks to Joyce Arroyo for all of her help in testing recipes,
for sharing her favorite recipes, and most of all,
for her enthusiasm with this project.*

*Thanks go also to Clorie Denmark,
who helped to keep me sane during the testing process.*

*As always, my husband and three daughters deserve special thanks
for their patience and support — and
their consumption of flatbreads for three meals a day!*

INTRODUCTION

Flatbreads are traditionally used as edible plates. For example, pizzas are nothing more than toppings piled on top of a "flatbread." In ancient times, nomads would make their bread and use it to either scoop up their food or to pile the meat, cheese and vegetables on top for eating. If you stop to think about it, edible plates are really quite efficient — think of all the dishes that do not have to be washed!

There are any number of foods eaten around the world that use this same general concept of wrapping the filling with an edible holder. Puerto Ricans use grated yucca roots for pasteles, Japanese use sheets of dried seaweed or a thin wrapper made primarily from eggs (egg rolls), and Greeks and Turks use grape leaves. Technically, an Italian ravioli is a wrapped food, but it is cooked by boiling. I made a distinction, therefore, in how the food was cooked, and used only grain-based wrappers in this book.

Ethnic flatbreads have been developed over thousands of years using local ingredients. It is no small surprise that the Aztec Indians would have used corn as a basic ingredient for their flatbread, the tortilla. East Indians, on the other hand, use wheat for their chapati and other breads. Ethiopians use teff for their injera. Rye grows well in the colder northern European climate and is the basis for many Norwegian, Swedish and Icelandic breads.

Many ethnic breads combine the grain with little more than water, salt and sometimes oil. Some breads are leavened with baking powder. Others trace their histories back to sourdough leavening and may now use commercially prepared yeast for a faster and more consistent leavening process.

How the breads are cooked varies according to their origins, which relate directly to the lifestyles of the people. Many ethnic breads are baked on griddles, or are fried, steamed or oven-baked. Baked breads may originally have been made in specially created ovens (such as Indian tandoors), suggesting a stable, rather than nomadic, life. Whatever their origins, ethnic breads may be easily made in any kitchen today.

A book on flatbreads from around the world should certainly contain a recipe for matzo, the unleavened cracker-like bread traditionally eaten during Jewish Passover. After a great deal of research, I have found no information on how to make this traditional flatbread. References say that it is made only with water and flour, but some recent versions have added egg, apple juice and flavorings. Matzo is made by several large commercial food producers in the United States, and is so readily available no one seems interested in making it at home.*

*My special thanks to Rabbi Ira Book and to Helen Winsten of Temple Beth Sholom for their assistance and advice.

EQUIPMENT

The early nomads carried very little in the way of cooking equipment. As a result, the equipment required to make many of these breads is minimal. However, if you really get into it, there are all kinds of neat kitchen gadgets that are designed specifically for or are helpful in making flatbreads.

Tortilla presses are not just for tortillas! Tortilla presses are handy gadgets for any recipe which requires the dough to be formed into small rounds. I use a press for chapatis, Icelandic flatbreads, Chinese pancakes, etc.

Electric tortilla presses are a combination of the hand presses and small electric griddles. The press is preheated and the dough is then flattened between the palm of your hands and placed on the press. The press heats the dough as it presses it. Because of this, doughs made from (corn) masa should only be pressed once, and that should be done very quickly. It takes some getting used to, but once you have developed the knack, it is the easiest and quickest way to make tortillas. Wheat-based tortillas may be pressed several times. While both sides of the press are warmed, the tortilla (or other flatbread) is generally cooked only on the bottom piece. This is to prevent steam from building in the tortilla, and it allows the tortilla to bubble and form layers. Round breads which are to be cooked until crisp (Icelandic flatbreads, for example) work quite nicely when cooked in the electric press with the lid closed right on the flatbread.

Hand tortilla presses are used for flattening a ball of dough into approximately a 6-inch round. For best results, place waxed paper or plastic bags between the press and the dough to prevent sticking. The dough may be pressed several times to obtain a thinner round, even if using (corn) masa.

Electric griddles are wonderful for any of the recipes that are cooked on a griddle. There is no need to grease the griddles as they generally have a nonstick coating.

Crepe pans are used for crepes as well as Ethiopian injera. They may also be used for large pancakes. Crepe pans have flat bottoms and slightly raised sides which make it easy to turn the crepe over. Season according to the directions that come with the pan. Nonstick pans may generally be used if properly seasoned. In general, spray the bottom of the pan with a nonstick vegetable spray. Prior to cooking the first crepe, melt ½ tsp. butter in the pan and swirl it around. It should not be necessary to melt butter after the first crepe.

Pastry cloths, marble boards and **marble rolling pins** are great for rolling out the doughs used in any of the meat- or cheese-filled empanada, borek or pastry recipes. The pastry cloths have flour rubbed into them which prevents the dough from sticking. The extra flour does not become kneaded into the dough, which could toughen the dough slightly. Marble that has been refrigerated also prevents the dough from sticking. Rounds may be cut with the dough directly on the cloth or the marble board.

Dumpling presses are wonderful little gadgets for filling pastries. The dough is rolled out on the pastry cloth, marble board or a lightly floured work surface and then cut into rounds using a biscuit cutter or similar sized round cutter (an empty tuna fish can, a cup or glass, etc.). Dumpling presses call for a round of just over 3½ inches in diameter, while most biscuit cutters are 3 inches. I find that if I roll the dough into a thin rectangle, cut the rounds with a biscuit cutter and then roll each round with a rolling pin, the rounds fit perfectly and the dough is thin yet still holds together well for sealing. The thinly rolled round is placed on the dumpling press and the filling is placed in the center of the round. By closing the press, the filling is encased and the dough is tightly sealed closed. The resulting pastries are uniformly sized and shaped, and present a professional appearance.

Deep fat fryers are not necessary but are nice for those few times a recipe is fried. They are generally inexpensive and the oil may be reused several times.

Pizza stones are great for making pizzas or pitas. Generally the dough is placed directly on the stone by sliding it from a peel. The bottoms of the breads tend to be crispier because the stones absorb excess moisture from the oven.

Also useful is a **cast iron skillet**. For years cast iron has been used for baking directly on fires. Breads such as *Indian Buckskin Bread* or *Egyptian Barley Bread* are especially good when baked in a very hot oven in a cast iron skillet. In fact, these recipes were tested using a 9-inch round pan, but the results did not even compare. Of course, you would not dream of baking in any other kind of skillet as the handle would probably melt!

Finally, kitchen appliances convenient for kneading dough make yeast doughs easy to make.

DIRECTIONS FOR MAKING YEAST-LEAVENED DOUGHS

BY HAND: Mix together flour and dry ingredients (salt, sugar and dry yeast) in a large bowl and make a well in the center. Mix together warm liquid (usually water) and other wet ingredients and pour into the well. Knead ingredients together by hand for 5 to 10 minutes until a soft, smooth dough is formed. Place the dough in a greased bowl, cover with a kitchen towel and place in a warm, draft-free location for about 1 hour unless otherwise directed.

BY HEAVY-DUTY MIXER OR DOUGH MAKER: Place ingredients in the work bowl following manufacturer's directions for a yeast bread. Knead dough for 6 to 8 minutes. Transfer dough to a large greased bowl, cover with a kitchen towel and place in a warm, draft-free location for 1 hour.

BY BREAD MACHINE: Place ingredients in the inner pan of your machine following manufacturer's directions. Select "dough cycle" on the bread machine. Allow dough to rise in the machine until dough cycle is complete. If using a DAK or Welbilt ABM 100, allow the machine to knead the dough the first time and leave in the machine to rise for 1 hour. Remove dough before the second kneading.

BY FOOD PROCESSOR: Mix dry ingredients together in the work bowl with the steel blade. Add liquid ingredients to bowl through the feed tube while the machine is running. Dough should form a ball which does not stick to the sides of the bowl. Knead for 1 to 2 minutes, transfer to a large greased bowl, cover with a kitchen towel and place in a warm, draft-free location for 1 hour.

INGREDIENTS

In developing the recipes for this book, I diligently tried to keep the flavor of the traditional bread. I came up with a recipe that worked best for me on a consistent basis and then, perhaps, started adding herbs and spices to make a simple bread into a gourmet bread.

When developing toppings or fillings to be used with a particular bread, I began to cross over the traditional, cultural methods for using the flatbreads. For example, tortillas are often used by Mexicans to make baked enchiladas. Orientals use fried egg roll wrappers. The reason Orientals fry their egg rolls and Mexicans bake their enchiladas has to do with their individual histories and cultures, not because the food tastes better one way or the other. So, why can't Oriental "egg rolls" be served as "baked enchiladas"? The answer is that they can. Virtually any filling can be simply wrapped in a warm, fresh tortilla, placed in the hollow pocket of a pita bread, or wrapped in a pastry-like empanada bread. Many of the fillings can be made in advance and eaten cold or warmed. Or they can be placed in the tortilla, pita or empanada bread wrapping and baked or fried. One simple topping or filling recipe can be served in a virtually unlimited manner.

Many ingredients are used in traditional baking worldwide. For example, cilantro is used by Mexicans, Orientals and Brazilians in their cooking. Coconut is used anywhere it grows, such as Hawaii, the Caribbean, Brazil and Indonesia. Seafood is also used in many of these countries. One would expect to (and does) find a variety of seafood recipes using both coconut and cilantro. What may vary is the method of serving. Indonesians or Hawaiians may traditionally serve their food on or with rice. Orientals may wrap their food in egg rolls and fry them. Brazilians may encase the food in a pastry-like dough for empadinhas. Mexicans may wrap the food in tortillas, cover with a sauce and bake as enchiladas.

Combining the spices and flavoring of one traditional food type with the method of preparing another traditional food can be a tremendous amount of fun! Indian enchiladas use a tomato sauce made with curry instead of the traditional Mexican tomato sauce. When serving the enchiladas, your family and guests will expect a Mexican meal but will identify it as Indian with the first bite!

Onions, garlic and herbs may generally be adjusted to suit your taste. If a recipe calls for $1/4$ cup diced onions, for example, you could use a couple of slices or, if you truly love onions, you could use $1/2$ an onion.

Grocery stores now carry minced garlic in jars (in the produce section). I use 1 tsp. prepared minced garlic to equate to 1 clove. It is easy to keep on hand, gives a fresher flavor than garlic powder and does not have the mess of mincing! I also tend to use the jars of jalapeños and ginger which are located in the same area. If your store does not carry these, ask them to or check other grocery stores.

Fresh cilantro (also known as coriander leaves or Chinese parsley) is used for cooking in many parts of the world. Over the past several years it has become much more accepted in American cooking and is now found in just about every grocery store produce section. Tear off only the leaves and chop or cut with scissors. Keep the fresh cilantro stems in a cup of water in the refrigerator, as it will last longer that way. Of course if you have it in a garden, you can cut it as you need it. Dried cilantro may be found in the spice section but the dried cilantro has very little flavor and should really be avoided.

Many of the recipes in this book use a ground version of a meat (lamb, beef, turkey, etc.) as I find it very easy and quick to work with. Most of the recipes call for you to mix the marinade, onions, garlic or any spices into the meat and allow it to sit in the refrigerator for 1 to 8 hours. Any of these recipes may be mixed and cooked immediately if desired.

Masa harina is a corn flour milled from lime-soaked corn, which is what gives it the traditional "tortilla" flavor. Masa, masa harina or maseca may be found in some large grocery stores, mail order catalogs, or in Mexican or specialty grocery stores.

GRIDDLE FLATBREADS

There are several different types of flatbreads used throughout the world, leavened and unleavened, which are cooked on a griddle or in a skillet. The history of these breads dates back to when they were baked on fires. Most flatbreads use a wheat flour, but some use corn or garbanzo (chickpea) flours and some are similar to pancakes.

In general, breads made on the griddle are served warm. The dough may be made in advance if necessary and refrigerated for several hours. Bring it up to room temperature prior to cooking. If the breads are made in advance, wrap in napkins or a kitchen towel and then in aluminum foil and keep (or place to rewarm) in a warm (100° to 150°) oven until ready to serve.

Tortillas, which are certainly griddle flatbreads, have become such a large category I have given them a chapter of their own, beginning on page 47.

CHAPATI

This typical Indian bread is often served with curry dishes and is always served warm. There is a special flour called chapati (or ata) flour which is a very finely ground flour with just a little bran in it. I have tried to accomplish the same taste by combining an all-purpose flour with the bran. Use a soft wheat bran (millers bran) and not a wheat bran cereal, which would be too coarse. Chapati are generally oval-shaped, but if you are using a tortilla maker, they may be round.

1¾ cups all-purpose flour
¼ cup wheat bran
½ tsp. salt

1 tbs. vegetable oil, or *Ghee*, page 14
⅔-¾ cup water
ghee or melted butter or oil for brushing

Mix dry ingredients together in a large bowl and set aside. Add oil to water and blend into dry ingredients. Knead until smooth. If using a machine (dough machine, bread machine, heavy duty mixer or food processor) to mix dough, add water mixture slowly as machine is kneading. Dough should be fairly soft. Place dough in an oiled bowl, cover tightly with plastic wrap and let rest for 30 to 40 minutes. Divide dough into 8 balls and flatten into 5- to 6-inch ovals, dusting the work surface and/or dough lightly if necessary. Pat dough between your hands several times. Heat griddle or cast

CHAPATI

iron skillet until it is very hot and then turn heat down to medium. Cook briefly on each side until bubbly and brown. If you have a grill or gas stove, you may place chapati directly over the flame very briefly to brown and puff. Brush warm chapati with ghee, melted butter or oil, stack and wrap in a kitchen towel or napkin to keep warm. A tortilla press may be used to flatten chapati (and cook, if electric). Makes 8.

GHEE

Many Indian recipes call for canola or other vegetable oil, but ghee (clarified butter) is the traditional oil used. It is really quite simple to clarify butter to make ghee for an authentic Indian flavor.

Melt 1 lb. unsalted butter in a heavy (cast iron) saucepan or skillet over low heat. Simmer uncovered for about 30 minutes. Strain through several (3 or 4) thicknesses of cheesecloth, making sure that none of the solids pass through. Store cooled ghee in a covered glass jar in a cool, dry location.

CHAPATI

INDIAN BEEF

This recipe combines traditional Indian spicing with the ease of ground meat (lamb, beef or turkey may be used). Serve wrapped in chapiti or parathas with slices of onion and tomatoes. Top with yogurt (seasoned or plain).

1 tbs. vegetable oil
1/4 cup lemon juice
1/4 medium onion, finely chopped
2 tsp. minced garlic
1 tsp. freshly grated ginger root

1 tsp. black pepper
1/2 tsp. salt
1/2-1 tsp. dried red pepper flakes
2 tsp. paprika
1 lb. ground meat

In a medium plastic or glass bowl, combine all ingredients except meat, mixing until well blended. Using your hands, blend meat into marinade mixture. Cover and refrigerate from 1 to several hours. Cook meat mixture in a large skillet, crumbling it as it cooks, until done. Spoon into chapati and top with slices of onions, tomatoes, hot peppers and yogurt, or toppings of your choice. Makes about 2 cups.

PARATHAS

A twist on chapati, parathas are brushed with oil or melted butter (traditionally clarified butter or ghee is used) during the cooking process. This results in a lighter, softer bread. Keep covered and warm until ready to serve with curry dishes.

1¾ cups all-purpose flour
¼ cup wheat bran
½ tsp. salt

3 tbs. canola, vegetable oil or ghee
½-⅔ cup water
oil or ghee for brushing

Mix dry ingredients together in a large bowl and set aside. Add oil to water and blend into dry ingredients. Knead until smooth. If using a machine (dough machine, bread machine, heavy duty mixer or food processor) to mix dough, add water mixture slowly as machine kneads. Dough should be fairly soft. Place dough in an oiled bowl, cover tightly with plastic wrap and let rest for 30 to 40 minutes. Form dough into 8 balls and flatten into 5- to 6-inch ovals, dusting the work surface and/or dough lightly if necessary. Brush dough with oil or ghee. Fold the 4 sides of the circle into the center and roll back into a circle. Repeat the process three more times, brushing with oil or ghee each time. This process layers oil or ghee in dough. Pat dough between your hands several times. Heat the griddle or cast iron skillet until it is very hot, and then turn heat down to medium. Brush each side of paratha with ghee before you cook it. Cook briefly on each side until bubbly and brown. Makes 8.

POTATO-STUFFED PARATHAS

*Parathas may be found stuffed with anything from vegetables or meats to herbs (which may also simply be added to the dough!). Add 1/2 lb. farmers cheese to this filling and wrap in **Turnover Pastry Dough, Yeast**, page 139. This is similar to Russian piroshki.*

2 medium baking potatoes
1 tbs. olive oil
1 tsp. lime juice
1 tbs. chopped fresh cilantro leaves, or
  1 tsp. dried

1-2 tbs. finely chopped onion
1/2 tsp. salt
1 tsp. pepper
dash freshly grated ginger root

Peel and cook potato until soft. Mash with oil and lime juice. Add remaining ingredients. Place in the refrigerator for an hour or more to develop flavors.

Make parathas as directed on page 16. On final rolling of dough, add 1/2 tbs. filling. Bring sides up to encase filling, roll the final time and cook as directed. Makes 1 cup.

ICELANDIC FLATBREAD

*These flatbreads are reminiscent of **Norwegian Flatbröds** (page 22) in that the flours are the same. These flatbreads, however, are meant to be eaten warm and soft.*

1 cup rye flour
1 cup whole wheat flour
½ cup all-purpose flour
2 tsp. baking powder
½ tsp. salt
1 cup water

In a large mixing bowl (or dough machine, bread machine, heavy duty mixer or food processor), combine flours, baking powder and salt. Slowly add water and knead until dough is smooth. Form into 15 to 18 golf ball-sized balls. Flatten each with a rolling pin or a tortilla press into a thin 6- to 7-inch circle. Cook over medium heat on an ungreased griddle or in an electric tortilla press until they are speckled and done, about 1 minute on each side. Makes 15 to 18.

ICELANDIC FLATBREAD

REUBEN TACOS

Icelandic Flatbreads are traditionally served warm with butter as an accompaniment to a meal. This recipe uses the flatbreads in a manner similar to tortillas. The flavors blend with the rye and whole wheat flavors for some interesting and delightful "tacos." As with any taco or tortilla, use as much or as little of the fillings as desired — the amounts given are guidelines for each individual taco.

Thousand Island dressing, or Dijon mustard or Russian salad dressing
1-2 slices Swiss cheese
2-3 slices corned beef
1-2 slices pastrami, optional
sauerkraut

Spread salad dressing over entire flatbread. Layer cheese and meats and top with sauerkraut. Fold bread in half and eat as a soft taco.

WEST INDIAN ROTI

Roti are traditionally served as an accompaniment to curry dishes, or they may be stuffed. The rolling and folding of the roti with oil or butter provides the flakiness.

2 cups all-purpose flour
1 tsp. baking powder
½ tsp. salt

about ¾ cup cold water
corn oil or melted butter as needed

Mix dry ingredients together in a large bowl. Continue to mix ingredients as you add water, adding only enough to make a stiff dough. Place dough in an oiled bowl, cover and let rest for about 20 minutes.

Form dough into 5 or 6 balls and flatten each one with a rolling pin or a tortilla press. Spread corn oil or melted butter on top of the round and then fold the circle back up into a ball by bringing the sides into the center. Place these balls back into the oiled bowl once more and let rest for another 10 to 15 minutes. Roll each ball back into a very thin round and brush both sides with corn oil or melted butter. Cook on a hot griddle for about 6 to 7 minutes, turning roti frequently. Upon removing the roti from the griddle, clap it between your hands two or three times or hit it with a wooden mallet several times to help make it flaky. Wrap roti in a clean kitchen towel to keep warm until serving. Makes 5 or 6.

WEST INDIAN ROTI

WEST INDIAN CHICKEN CURRY

*This particular curry recipe is based on one from Guyana and is adapted to a simple marinade. Instead of cooking an entire chicken, I have opted to use ground chicken or turkey, which I wrap in the roti, much like a soft taco. This same recipe may be used as a filling for the roti following the directions for **Potato-Stuffed Parathas**, page 17. For a Caribbean flavor, serve with mango chutney, available in many grocery or gourmet stores.*

1 lb. ground chicken or turkey
1/4-1/2 medium onion, finely chopped
2-3 tsp. minced garlic
2-4 tbs. fresh cilantro leaves
1 tsp. turmeric

1/2 tsp. cumin
1/2 tsp. cayenne pepper
2 tsp. freshly grated ginger root
salt and pepper to taste

Mix all ingredients together until well blended. Cook immediately or refrigerate for 1 to several hours. The longer it sits, the more flavor is developed. Cook meat in a large skillet in a very small amount of oil until no longer pink. Serve wrapped in roti. Makes about 2 cups.

NORWEGIAN FLATBRÖD

Flatbröds are crisp, cracker-like breads that are dried and may be kept for long periods of time. Many "loaves" are circular with holes in the middle, which is how they are hung on lines to dry. Pricking the dough with a fork prevents the bread from puffing during baking.

1 cup water
2 tbs. butter
½ tsp. salt

1 cup rye flour
¾ cup all-purpose flour
¾ cup whole wheat or barley flour

In a medium saucepan, bring water to a boil, add butter and stir until butter melts. Pour mixture into a large mixing bowl. Combine salt and flours together and slowly add flours to water, mixing well. Initially, a hand mixer will help blend flour and water, but eventually dough will have to be kneaded by hand on a floured work surface. Dough should be fairly firm and should hold together nicely. Divide dough into approximately 12 pieces and roll each one into a thin circle or press with a tortilla press. Prick rounds all over with a fork. Bake on a hot griddle for 10 to 15 minutes on each side. Rounds should be lightly browned and crisp. Cool on a wire rack and store in an airtight container. Makes 12.

NORWEGIAN FLATBRÖD

TIP: If using an electric tortilla press, press once very quickly, turn dough over and press again. Keep cover closed to crisp bread, and watch carefully.

CRAB DIP

*This recipe may be used as a dip with pieces of **Norwegian Flatbröds** or it may be spooned into **Icelandic Flatbreads**, page 18, and served as soft tacos.*

6 oz. crabmeat
8 oz. cream cheese, softened
1 tbs. milk
1 tsp. lemon juice
½ tsp. horseradish

1 tbs. finely chopped onion
1 tbs. chopped fresh parsley, or 1 tsp. dried
salt and pepper to taste

Combine all ingredients using an electric mixer. Place in a greased casserole and bake for about 20 minutes in a preheated 350° oven. Makes about 2 cups.

NAVAJO FRIED BREAD

Like many ethnic flatbreads, these breads are traditionally used as edible plates. The dough may be flattened into circles with a rolling pin or a tortilla press.

2 cups all-purpose flour (unbleached)
2 tsp. baking powder
½ tsp. salt

4 tbs. butter, margarine or shortening
½-⅔ cup water
canola or vegetable oil for frying

Mix dry ingredients together. Cut in butter by hand or with a pastry blender until mixture has the texture of cornmeal. Slowly add water and mix until dough comes together. Knead for about 3 minutes. Cover dough with a kitchen towel and let it rest for about 15 minutes. Form dough into 6 equal balls, cover and let rest for another 10 minutes. Flatten each ball into a 6- or 7-inch circle and make a long cut down the center of the circle with a very sharp knife or razor blade. Using a large skillet (I use cast iron) with about an inch of canola or other vegetable oil, fry one bread at a time in very hot oil (380° to 400°). Cook for 1 minute on each side and drain on paper towels. Keep bread wrapped and warm for serving. Makes 6.

TIP: If you prefer, this bread may be baked on a griddle or electric tortilla press. While it is not traditional, you still get some of the flavor without the added fat.

NAVAJO FRIED BREAD

NAVAJO TOSTADA

The Navajo Indians use their fried breads to hold foods, much like tostadas. Put out warm Navajo bread and bowls of toppings and let everyone make his or her own "tostada" — a favorite for people of all ages.

shredded lettuce
chopped tomatoes
diced onions
diced hot peppers
grated cheese (Monterey Jack works well)
beans

TIP: This bread is an excellent snack served with jam or honey. Or, sprinkle with cinnamon sugar (¼ cup sugar and 1 tbs. cinnamon) for a different delicious treat.

NAAN

This version of an East Indian, white flour flatbread is cooked directly on a griddle or electric tortilla press and is quite easy to make. The longer the dough sits, the more flavor it seems to develop. It can easily be made in the morning and refrigerated for an evening meal.

2 cups all-purpose flour
1½ tsp. baking powder
1 tsp. sugar
½ tsp. salt

¾ cup plain nonfat yogurt
2 tbs. vegetable oil
2 tbs. water or less, to adjust
   consistency of dough

Mix together flour, baking powder, sugar and salt in a large bowl and make a well in the center. Mix together yogurt and oil and pour into well. Knead ingredients together for 10 to 15 minutes, adding water only if and as necessary until a soft, smooth dough is formed. Place dough in a greased bowl, cover with a kitchen towel and place in a warm, draft-free location for 2 hours.

Form dough into 5 or 6 balls and flatten each ball by hand into a 6-inch circle or oval. Cook on a griddle for 1 or 2 minutes on each side, flipping frequently. The resulting bread is similar to a tortilla and may be used in the same way. Makes 5 or 6.

NAAN

TANDOORI CHICKEN

This chicken is traditionally roasted whole in the tandoor oven. This version uses the basic tandoori marinade with boneless chicken breasts, which are grilled.

MARINADE

2 tbs. lemon juice
2 cups plain nonfat yogurt
2-3 tsp. freshly grated ginger root
2 cloves garlic
1 tsp. cayenne pepper, or to taste

2 tsp. paprika
1 tsp. ground coriander
1 tsp. ground cumin
$\frac{1}{2}$ tsp. salt
1 tsp. coarsely ground black pepper

1 lb. boneless chicken breasts (3 or 4)
onion slices, tomato slices and chopped green chiles for filling

Mix all marinade ingredients until very well blended. Pour over chicken breasts in a glass or plastic bowl and refrigerate for 1 to several hours. Remove chicken and reserve marinade. Grill chicken over medium heat until done. To make yogurt sauce, simmer reserved marinade over low heat for about 5 minutes or heat in the microwave on HIGH for 2 minutes, stirring occasionally. Once chicken has been cooked, cut into bite-sized pieces, toss with warm yogurt sauce and wrap in naan with onion, tomato and hot peppers. Makes 5 or 6.

CHINESE PANCAKES

These pancakes are traditionally brushed with hoisin or plum sauce and used to wrap pieces of Peking Duck, scallion and cucumber.

2 cups all-purpose flour
1 tbs. sesame oil
½-⅔ cups hot water
2-4 tbs. sesame oil for brushing

Place flour in a large bowl and slowly mix in oil and water until you have a smooth dough. Knead dough for about 5 minutes and let rest for about 10 minutes. Roll dough into a thin rectangle and jelly-roll it into a tight rope shape. Cut rope into 12 equal pieces. Roll each piece into a round, about 7 inches in diameter. Brush tops of pancakes with sesame oil and press 2 together, oiled side to oiled side. Cook on a very hot griddle or electric tortilla press. Turn and cook the other side when pancake starts to bubble and brown spots appear on the bottom. Peel pancakes apart and fold each pancake in half with the oiled side in. Wrap in a napkin or kitchen towel and place on a plate in a warm oven until served. Makes 12.

CHINESE PANCAKES

PLUM CHICKEN

This is an easy substitute for Peking Duck, which may be served wrapped in **Chinese Pancakes**. *I make the marinade ahead of time and start the chicken marinating in the morning as I'm getting the kids off to school.*

MARINADE

1 jar (6.5 oz.) plum or duck sauce
1 tbs. hoisin sauce
1 tbs. soy sauce
2 tbs. sesame oil

1 tsp. freshly grated ginger root
1-2 tsp. minced garlic
¼ cup fresh cilantro leaves
cayenne pepper to taste

1 lb. boneless chicken breasts, cut into bite-sized pieces

Mix marinade ingredients together in a food processor. Combine with chicken in a glass or plastic bowl, cover and place in the refrigerator for 6 to 8 hours. Remove chicken from marinade and reserve. Heat 1 tbs. sesame oil in a large skillet or wok and stir-fry chicken. Add marinade and cook until chicken is no longer pink. Makes 10 to 12 servings with pancakes.

CHINESE ONION PANCAKES

Onion pancakes are often served with stir-fry. The onions are traditionally folded into the dough just before cooking. This version incorporates the diced onions right into the dough for simplicity.

2 cups all-purpose flour
dash salt
2 green onions, green part only, finely chopped
1 tbs. sesame oil
½-⅔ cup warm water

In a large bowl, combine flour, salt and green onions. Slowly mix in oil and then water, until you have a smooth, slightly sticky dough. Cover and let rest for about 10 minutes. Divide dough into 12 equal pieces and roll into rounds about 5 or 6 inches in diameter. Cook on a very hot, ungreased griddle or in an electric tortilla press. Makes 12.

CHINESE ONION PANCAKES

ORIENTAL SHRIMP

This easy recipe may be put together at the last minute for a quick meal or for entertaining. I whirl the shrimp in the food processor for just a second to coarsely chop into bite-sized pieces, which are easier to eat in the pancake.

MARINADE

¼ cup fresh cilantro leaves (more or less)
2 tbs. soy sauce
2 tbs. rice wine vinegar
1 tbs. lime juice

2 tbs. sesame oil
1 tbs. brown sugar
salt to taste
red and/or black pepper to taste

1 lb. cleaned shrimp
½ cup snow peas

2 tbs. sesame oil

Mix marinade ingredients together in a blender or food processor until cilantro is finely chopped and all ingredients are well blended. Place shrimp and snow peas in marinade and refrigerate for at least 2 hours. In a large skillet or wok, heat 2 tbs. sesame oil and stir-fry shrimp and snow peas with marinade sauce. Wrap in *Chinese Onion Pancakes*. Makes 10 to 12 servings with pancakes.

ETHIOPIAN INJERA

Teff is native to Northern Africa and is the grain used by Ethiopians in preparing their fermented, spongy flatbread. Pieces of injera are used as edible utensils to scoop up their spicy meals, often a very spicy stew called **Wats***, page 33. Injera has a very strong flavor.*

1 cup teff flour
1½ cups water
½ tsp. salt

Mix flour and water together in a large bowl, loosely cover and allow to sit at room temperature for 12 to 24 hours. Pour off any liquid that rises to the top and stir in the salt. Pour a scant ½ cup batter into a crepe pan or seasoned skillet and cook over medium heat for about 3 minutes on each side. Makes 2 to 3.

ETHIOPIAN INJERA

WATS

Ethiopians use a spice mixture called berbere to flavor their foods, including this version of their staple stew. Hard boiled eggs may also be added to the stew towards the end of the simmering.

1 medium onion, diced
2 tsp. minced garlic
4 tbs. butter or margarine
1 can (6 oz.) tomato paste
1 lb. chicken, cut into bite-sized pieces
1 tsp. freshly grated ginger root

1-1½ tbs. cayenne pepper, to taste
dash ground cloves
¼ tsp. cinnamon
½ tsp. black pepper
about 1 cup water

In a skillet, cook onion and garlic in butter until they just begin to soften. Stir in tomato paste, chicken and spices. Stir to coat chicken completely with tomato paste mixture. Add water as you continue to stir. Simmer over low heat for 30 to 40 minutes. Makes 4 to 5 servings.

DANISH FLATBRÖD

Unlike **Norwegian Flatbröd**, *which is dry and much like a cracker,* **Danish Fladbröd** *is more like an oatmeal pancake. It may be eaten with butter and maple syrup (or honey) or it may be spread with a thick, creamy, sweet filling and rolled for eating. Oat flour may easily be made by grinding regular or instant oats in a blender or food processor, one cup at a time.*

1½ cups oat flour
1 cup all-purpose flour
1 tsp. baking soda

½ tsp. salt
3 tbs. canola or vegetable oil
⅔ cup buttermilk

Mix all dry ingredients together in a large bowl. Add oil to measured buttermilk and blend into dry ingredients, mixing well. Knead dough on floured counter until it has formed a soft, smooth ball. Continue to knead for 5 more minutes. Form dough into 8 equal balls. Flatten each ball with a rolling pin or a tortilla press until each one is as thin as possible. Cook on a lightly greased, hot griddle until brown spots appear, about 3 minutes. Makes 8.

SOCCA

These crisp, spicy pancake breads are common in the Mediterranean area. They are often broken into sticks, fried in deep fat much like French fries, and served with meat. They may also be sold by street vendors and eaten with salt and pepper for a simple snack. Garbanzo flour is marketed by Arrowhead Mills and may be found in health food stores. As a variation, try substituting freshly ground red pepper or a multi-pepper blend for the black pepper.

¾ cup garbanzo flour
½ tsp. salt
¼ tsp. coarsely ground black pepper, or
  to taste

1 tbs. olive oil
½ cup water
additional olive oil for brushing
additional salt and pepper to taste

Combine flour, salt and pepper. Add oil and then water to form a thick batter. Pour into a large (10-inch) greased cast iron skillet so that it barely covers the bottom of the pan. Bake in a preheated 450° oven for 5 minutes and remove. Switch the baking control to broil. Using a pastry brush, spread olive oil on top of bread and return pan to oven so that the bread is close to the broiler. Broil for 2 to 3 minutes until bread is crisp. Watch closely to avoid burning. Serve with salt and pepper sprinkled on top, if desired. Makes 2.

ATAÏF

These Middle Eastern sweet breads are a cross between pancakes and crepes. They are traditionally served with an orange blossom syrup, cream and chopped nuts, or they are stuffed with a cheese mixture and fried.

1½ tsp. dry yeast
1 cup all-purpose flour
1 tsp. sugar
1 cup lukewarm water

In a large bowl, mix yeast with flour and sugar. Add water slowly, stirring until a smooth, liquid batter is obtained. Cover with a kitchen towel and place in a warm, draft-free location for about 1 hour.

Using a paper towel, spread a very thin coat of vegetable oil in the bottom of a heavy, cast iron skillet. Heat pan until it is very hot and then reduce heat to medium. Pour 3 or 4 tbs. batter into the pan and, using the back of a spoon, spread it around a little but not too thinly. When the top of the "pancake" becomes bubbly and lifts easily, turn it over and cook the other side. Makes approximately 8.

ATAÏF

ATAÏF TOPPINGS

Ataïfs are traditionally served with Orange Blossom Syrup. Orange blossom water may be purchased in some gourmet shops or by mail order. Any fruit-flavored syrup complements the ataïf. The ataïf is dipped in the cold syrup, cream (whipped or heavy) is poured over that and the whole thing is topped with finely ground pistachios or almonds.

Orange Blossom Syrup

1 cup sugar
2/3 cup water

1 tsp. lemon juice
1 tsp. orange blossom water

heavy cream or whipped cream

chopped pistachios, almonds or walnuts

In a medium saucepan, dissolve sugar in water and lemon juice until it is thick enough to coat the back of a spoon. Stir in orange blossom water and simmer for 1 to 2 minutes. Allow to cool and refrigerate. Dip ataïf in syrup, cover with heavy cream or whipped cream and top with chopped pistachios, almonds or walnuts.

TIP: For a westernized version, top each ataïf with apricot syrup or apricot preserves, whipped cream and ground almonds or pistachios.

ATAÏF

STUFFED ATAÏF

Ataïf may found stuffed with a variety of fillings ranging from plain cheese to chopped nuts.

FILLINGS

- Use a scant tablespoon of ricotta, cheddar or mozzarella in the center of the ataïf.

- Or, sprinkle hot, fried ataïf with a scant tablespoon of very finely chopped nuts topped with a cinnamon sugar mixture ($1/4$ cup sugar with 2 tsp. cinnamon, or to taste).

When cooking the ataïf (see page 36), cook only one side. Place filling in the center of the uncooked side of ataïf and fold one side over so that filling is encased. Seal by pinching with your fingers. Fry in deep fat until golden brown.

BARLEY BREAD

This bread is enjoyed by Egyptians, Afghans, Indians and Northern Europeans. It is a slightly sweet bread that is usually smothered with butter, honey or preserves.

1½ cups barley flour
¾ cup all-purpose flour
1 tsp. baking powder
½ tsp. salt
1 tbs. sesame, anise or caraway seed
2 tbs. vegetable oil

2 tbs. honey
1 egg
1 cup milk
1-2 tbs. vegetable oil
2 tbs. melted butter for top of bread

Mix together all dry ingredients in a large bowl. In a separate bowl, combine 2 tbs. vegetable oil, honey, egg and milk. Add to dry ingredients, mixing until just blended. Do not overmix. Spread 1 to 2 tbs. vegetable oil on the bottom of a 9-inch cast iron skillet so that it is well coated. Pour thick batter into skillet and drizzle with melted butter. Bake in a well preheated 375° oven for about 35 to 45 minutes or until a toothpick inserted into the center comes out clean. Cut into wedges to serve. Makes 8 servings.

TIP: Serve barley bread with butter and any fruit preserves.

CREPES

*While many Americans often equate crepes with desserts, they may be enjoyed with a variety of fillings ranging from meats to cheeses to fruits. Crepes that are used to wrap the food inside (fold like **Burritos**, page 86) and then fried are referred to as blintzes. The first time you make a crepe or use a new crepe pan, you may have to experiment until you develop the right technique.*

½ cup all-purpose flour
1 egg
1 tbs. vegetable oil
½ tsp. vanilla extract, optional
1 cup milk (add more if the consistency is too thick)

Add ingredients to the work bowl of a food processor (use the steel blade) or blender in the order given. Add milk slowly as machine is running until you have a cream-like consistency with no lumps. Do not overmix. Pour about ¼ cup batter into a preheated crepe pan or a small seasoned, nonstick skillet. Tip skillet and swirl batter so that it spreads over bottom of pan. Cook over low heat for about 1 minute on each side. Turn crepe when the edges start to lift and are beginning to crisp. Makes 6 to 8.

CREPES

ORANGE CHEESE FILLING

*Whether you serve this rolled in a crepe (or **Danish Flatbröd**, page 34) or fry it in a blintz, this is a true delight.*

4 oz. cream cheese, softened
½ cup confectioners' sugar

4 mandarin orange segments
pinch orange peel

Beat softened cream cheese until creamy and blend in remaining ingredients. Serve wrapped in a crepe. Makes about 1 cup.

BLINTZ FILLING

Blintzes are usually associated with a cheese filling.

1 cup cottage cheese
1 egg
1 tsp. vanilla or almond extract

pinch salt
1 tbs. sugar

Combine all ingredients. Place a heaping tablespoon cheese filling in the (vertical) center of the crepe. Fold the bottom and the top over and then the two sides so that the cheese is completely encased. Fry lightly in 1 to 2 tbs. butter in a large skillet. The blintz should be light brown. Makes about 1¼ cups.

NORWEGIAN LEFSE (POTATO PANCAKES)

These potato pancakes are rolled very thinly. There are even special rolling pins which put designs into the pancake. Early Norwegian immigrants settled in the American Midwest where lefse are still often eaten and where it is an art (dying art) to make a perfect lefse. Lefse are generally eaten rolled with butter and cinnamon sugar.

1 cup all-purpose flour
1/2 tsp. salt
2 medium potatoes, cooked and mashed
2 tbs. melted butter
milk

In a large bowl, combine flour and salt. Mix in potatoes and melted butter until well blended. Add milk if necessary to obtain a soft, manageable dough. Break off egg-sized pieces and roll each piece until it is paper-thin. Cook on a hot, ungreased griddle until brown spots appear. Makes 6.

PANCAKES (AMERICAN)

The early New England settlers discovered how wonderful butter and maple syrup taste on these common flatbreads. Australians eat their pancakes with sugared strawberries and whipped cream.

1 cup all-purpose flour
1/2 tsp. salt
2 tbs. sugar
1 tsp. baking powder
1/2 tsp. baking soda
2 tbs. canola oil, vegetable oil or melted butter
1 egg, beaten
1 cup buttermilk

In a large bowl, blender container or food processor work bowl, mix together all dry ingredients. Add liquid ingredients until just blended in. Do not overmix. Drop by spoonfuls onto a hot griddle. Pancakes are done when bubbles appear on the surface and the bottom is lightly browned. Gently lift with a spatula to turn over. Makes 6 medium-sized pancakes.

JOHNNYCAKES

New England johnnycakes are made from a coarse stone-ground cornmeal sometimes called johnnycake meal. Like pancakes, johnnycakes are eaten with butter and maple syrup.

1 cup johnnycake meal, or stone-ground cornmeal
½ tsp. salt
2 tbs. maple syrup
¾ cup milk

In a large bowl by hand or with an electric mixer, combine cornmeal and salt. Add maple syrup and milk as you mix, until you have a lump-free, pourable batter. Pour a scant ¼ cup batter onto a medium hot, greased griddle and cook until lightly browned (the edges will start to brown, too). Flip with a spatula and cook the other side. Makes 4 to 6.

BLINIS

These Russian and Northern European "pancakes" are traditionally served with caviar and sour cream.

1½ tsp. dry yeast
¼ cup lukewarm water
1 cup buckwheat flour
½ cup all-purpose flour
½ tsp. salt

1 tbs. brown sugar
1 cup lukewarm milk
2 tbs. melted butter, cooled
2 eggs

Proof yeast in warm water for approximately 5 minutes. Meanwhile, in a large bowl, combine flours, salt and sugar. Add milk, butter and eggs to yeast mixture, blending briefly. Add this mixture into flour, mixing until well blended. Cover bowl with plastic wrap or a kitchen towel and let sit in a warm, draft-free location for 1 to 1½ hours. Drop by spoonfuls onto a hot griddle. Blinis are done when bubbles appear on the surface and the bottom is lightly browned. Gently lift with a spatula to turn over. Serve immediately. Makes 10 to 12.

BUCKSKIN BREAD

This American Indian bread uses a familiar blend of ingredients but is baked instead of being cooked on a griddle. This light-colored bread is perfect for picking up any sauces, gravies, etc.

2 cups all-purpose flour
1 tsp. baking powder
½ tsp. salt
1 tbs. sugar
¾-1 cup water

Combine dry ingredients and add water, mixing until you have a soft dough. Press into a greased 9-inch cast iron skillet and bake in a preheated 400° oven for 15 to 20 minutes. Cut into pie-shaped wedges to serve. Makes 6 to 8 servings.

TIP: This dough is very soft and sticky. Use wet hands when pressing the dough into the pan to avoid sticking.

TORTILLAS

One of the attractive things about tortillas is that they are so versatile. Any tortilla may be cooked or prepared as a taco, burrito, enchilada, etc. Similarly, any of the fillings listed in this chapter may be prepared in any number of methods. In this chapter, I have given general directions for preparing different kinds of meals using tortillas, as well as preparing individual fillings. For example, vary *Tropical Tacos* by making the recipe into enchiladas with a little cheese on top. Vary amounts of ingredients listed to suit your taste, or omit them entirely. There is no right or wrong when making a meal with tortillas.

Use these recipes to stimulate your imagination!

BASIC TORTILLA DIRECTIONS

1. Mix dry ingredients together. Mix wet ingredients together and add to dry ingredients. Knead until smooth, about 2 minutes. You will find baking powder listed as an optional ingredient in all tortilla recipes. I much prefer the results when using the baking powder in both masa- and wheat-based recipes.
2. Place dough in a greased bowl and cover tightly with plastic wrap directly on the dough, sealing it to prevent air from drying it out. As an alternative, place dough in a plastic bag.
3. Let dough rest like this for about an hour. If keeping dough for a longer period of time prior to making tortillas, lightly grease dough and place it in a tightly sealed plastic bag in the refrigerator for up to 24 hours.
4. Form dough into golf ball- or egg-sized pieces, making sure that remaining dough is covered at all times to prevent it from drying out. For corn (masa) tortillas, flatten each ball between the palms of your hands and return to the plastic bag for another 15- to 30-minute rest. Keep formed dough wrapped to prevent drying as you cook the others.
5. Flatten each ball in a tortilla press with a quick, gentle pressure. Too much pressure or too long a pressing in an electric tortilla press will cause the tortilla to split or become lacy. Corn tortillas have a greater tendency to do this than wheat tortillas. Wheat-based tortillas may be pressed two or three times in an

electric press. Tortillas may also be rolled into rounds between two pieces of waxed paper or plastic (produce bags from the grocery store work well). If the dough begins to dry out, mix in a teaspoon of water at a time to soften it.

6. Cook 1 to 2 minutes on each side on a hot griddle. If the griddle is a coated, nonstick material, it is not necessary to grease. If the griddle is uncoated, it is necessary to lightly grease for corn tortillas but not for wheat. Tortillas may also be baked in electric tortilla presses such as the Vitantonio *Tortilla Chef* or in an ungreased electric skillet heated to 375°. Overcooking will cause the tortilla to be crisp. Do not push down on the tortilla as it puffs because the puffing is what causes the layers to form.

7. Keep cooked tortillas warm and moist by wrapping in a kitchen towel or in a tortilla holder. The towel-wrapped tortillas may also be wrapped in aluminum foil and kept in a warm (150° to 200°) oven.

HOW TO SERVE TORTILLAS

Unless fried for tacos or tostadas, tortillas should be served warm and moist. If you have made your tortillas in advance, use any of the following methods to warm them for serving:

- Place two or three tortillas wrapped in a kitchen towel in a steamer basket over boiling water.
- Heat on a hot, ungreased griddle or in a hot, lightly greased frying pan for a few seconds until warm.
- Wrap the tortillas in slightly damp paper towels and microwave for 3 to 5 seconds per tortilla.
- Wrap the tortillas in slightly damp paper towels and then in aluminum foil. Heat in a warm oven (150° to 200°) for about 5 minutes.

Tortillas may be enjoyed all by themselves, or as a "plate" or holder for many different types of foods, whether they are filled to make enchiladas, or fried for tacos, tostadas or a taco salad bowl.

FRESH TORTILLA CHIPS

Try making chips from a variety of flavored and/or colored tortillas. Serve with salsa.

FRESH TORTILLA CHIPS

Cut each tortilla into wedges with a pizza wheel or scissors (like a pie) and fry in a full deep fryer or in ½ inch canola or vegetable oil in a skillet. Turn the wedges once and fry until crisp and golden. Place on paper towels to drain and sprinkle with salt if desired. (Try using jalapeño salt if you can find it!)

LOW FAT, BAKED CHIPS

Cut the fresh tortilla into wedges and place pieces on a perforated pizza pan that has been greased or lightly sprayed with nonstick cooking spray. Bake in a 500° oven until crisp, about 5 minutes. Salt if desired before or after baking.

FLAVORED CHIPS

Brush tortillas with oil or melted butter, and sprinkle with flavorings such as paprika, cumin or cinnamon. Cut into triangles and bake in a preheated 350° oven for 10 to 12 minutes.

FRESH TORTILLA CHIPS

SALSA CRUDA

One of the most common accompaniments to any tortilla dish is a salsa. There are many salsas available in the marketplace now and a number of them are quite good. I would be remiss, however, not to offer at least one salsa recipe for use with any tortilla recipes.

3 large, ripe tomatoes
1/2 cup fresh cilantro leaves
1/4-1/2 medium onion, coarsely chopped
finely chopped jalapeño to taste (I use about 1 tbs.)
1 tbs. lime juice

Cut tomatoes into quarters and process very briefly in a food processor one at a time until the tomatoes are just chopped. Mix together with all remaining ingredients and serve. The salsa may be refrigerated in a glass container for a day or two.

TACOS

Tacos are tortillas wrapped around any kind of fillings in addition to the traditional spiced ground meat, cheese, lettuce, tomatoes, etc. They may be either soft such as with fajitas (hot off the griddle), or crisply fried. Most Americans equate the U-shaped fried tortilla (taco) shells with tacos, although many Mexican restaurants offer the soft variety as well.

SOFT TACO DIRECTIONS

Place fillings in the center of a warm tortilla, and fold the tortilla in half over top of the filling.

CRISPY TACO DIRECTIONS

Heat about 1/2 inch oil in a large skillet. Place tortilla flat in skillet and heat until it is warm enough to fold. Using two forks, or tongs, fold one side loosely over on top of the other and continue to hold in place until tortilla begins to crisp. Using the forks, flip taco shell over and crisp the other side. Remove from heat, drain on paper towels and fill with desired ingredients.

TACOS

(CORN) MASA TORTILLAS

Masa harina is a special corn flour which is used to achieve the anticipated "tortilla taste." The corn is soaked in lime water prior to milling. Regular cornmeal or corn flour will not give the same flavor. Make sure to use warm water that is comfortable to the inside of your wrist (about 110° to 115°). Water too hot will make a hard, stiff tortilla. Makes about 10.

2 cups masa harina*
½ tsp. salt, optional
1 tsp. baking powder

1 tbs. vegetable or canola oil
1⅛-1¼ cups warm water

Follow directions for making tortillas beginning on page 49.

TIP: It takes practice to flatten these just right in an electric tortilla press. Use a larger egg-sized piece of dough than you would for a wheat tortilla and flatten it between your palms first. Place it on the press and very quickly press down. You cannot press it a second time or it will lace. Turn the tortilla over and bake the top side first and then the bottom side.

*Masa harina may be found in some large grocery stores as masa or maseca. It is also available in Mexican shops or through some mail order catalogs.

TACOS

TACO BUFFET

Whether you are serving dinner to a hungry family, to friends or to a group of birthday party guests, it is fun for individuals to make their own tacos. The tortillas can be either crisped or served soft and warm. I usually make several different tortilla doughs early in the day, refrigerate them and then make a fresh tortilla for each person when needed. Have plenty of filling ingredients on hand!

grated cheeses (sharp cheddar, Monterey/jalapeño Jack)
salsa (hot and/or mild)
ground meat seasoned with taco seasonings
shredded chicken or pork
beans (refried, black, pinto or kidney)
sliced onions
chopped tomatoes
shredded lettuce
sour cream
jalapeños or other peppers (habañeros, etc.)
finely chopped nuts (walnuts, almonds, pine nuts)
fresh herbs (cilantro, basil, parsley)

TACOS

SEASONED TACO MEAT

Either ground beef or turkey may be used with this homemade taco seasoning. Of course, if you prefer, you may simply purchase a packet of taco seasoning.

1 lb. ground meat
finely chopped jalapeños to taste
1 tsp. salt
1/4-1/2 tsp. garlic powder
1/2 tsp. onion powder
1 tsp. cumin
1 tsp. oregano
2 tsp. paprika
1/2-3/4 cup water

Brown meat in a large skillet and drain if necessary. Stir in seasonings and water and simmer over low heat for about 5 minutes. Use meat in tacos, burritos or enchiladas. Or for variety, use this meat as a filling for empanadas. Makes 2 cups.

TACOS

SHREDDED PORK

Whether in the American Southwest, Central or South America or the Caribbean, shredded pork is an integral part of the diet and is usually served wrapped in a tortilla or roti. Any type of pepper may be used. Since some peppers are hotter than others (habañeros, for example), adjust the number of peppers to your taste. Always wear gloves when working with hot peppers!

4-8 hot peppers
1-2 tsp. minced garlic
1 tbs. canola oil
1 tsp. salt
1 tbs. fresh oregano leaves, or 1 tsp. dried
1½ cups cold water, or ½ cup water plus more as needed
1 lb. boneless pork loin roast

Place peppers on an ungreased baking sheet and roast in a preheated 300° oven about 3 or 4 minutes. You'll know when they are ready by the aroma. Remove and allow to cool. Slice each pepper in half and remove stems and veins. The seeds are the hottest parts, so if you want it very spicy, leave them in. Otherwise, remove seeds too. Makes about 2½ cups.

TACOS

Place cleaned peppers, garlic, oil, salt and oregano in a food processor and process until finely chopped and blended. Stir this mixture into 1½ cups cold water and set aside.

Trim any fat from meat and cut into 1- or 2-inch cubes. Place meat in a large glass or plastic container with a lid and pour chile water over it to marinate. Cover mixture and refrigerate for 24 to 36 hours. When ready to cook, place meat and chile water in a roasting pan (no rack), cover and cook in a preheated 325° oven for approximately 2 hours.

An alternative cooking method is to cook meat in ½ cup water in a Dutch oven or very large skillet on top of the stove for 8 to 10 hours. Add water as needed. The meat is done (with either cooking method) when it is very tender and shreds easily. Shred meat by pulling off strands with a fork. Shredded meat may be warmed by heating it in the cooking juices.

Serve shredded pork wrapped in tortillas with cheddar or Jack cheese. Leftovers, if any, may be frozen or refrigerated.

TACOS

MARINATED PORK

*This is a quick and easy variation of the **Shredded Pork** recipe.*

1 lb. boneless pork loin roast
olive oil
2 tbs. minced garlic
1 tsp. onion powder, or ¼ cup minced onion
1 tbs. cumin

Coat pork with olive oil. Combine remaining ingredients and rub onto pork. Marinate for 2 to 3 hours. Cook meat in ½ cup water in a Dutch oven or very large skillet on top of the stove for 8 to 10 hours. Add water as needed. The meat is done when it is very tender and shreds easily. Shred meat by pulling off strands with a fork. Shredded meat may be warmed by heating it in the cooking juices. Makes about 2½ cups.

TACOS

CILANTRO TORTILLAS

Dried cilantro has very little flavor when compared to fresh. Use fresh cilantro which is available in most grocery stores in the produce section, often with the parsley. These tortillas make very flavorful chips. Serve with salsa.

2 cups all-purpose flour (unbleached)
½ tsp. salt
¼-⅓ cup fresh cilantro leaves
½ tsp. baking powder, optional
2 tbs. olive oil
⅔-¾ cup water

Follow directions for making tortillas beginning on page 49. Makes 12 to 15 tortillas.

TACOS

TROPICAL TACOS

This is a cross between a Brazilian and an Hawaiian seafood dish and is served wrapped in warm tortillas as a soft taco.

1-2 tbs. olive oil
½ medium red onion, chopped
1-2 cloves garlic, minced
1 lb. bay (small) scallops
1 tsp. freshly grated ginger root (about ½-inch slice)
¾-1 cup coconut milk, unsweetened
¼-⅓ cup chopped fresh cilantro, or Italian parsley
salt and pepper to taste

In a large skillet, heat olive oil. Sauté onion, garlic and scallops until onions are soft and scallops are cooked, about 10 minutes. Add ginger and coconut milk and simmer uncovered, stirring occasionally for 5 minutes. Add cilantro and season to taste. Makes 4 to 5 servings.

TIP: Chopped shrimp or boneless chicken breasts may be substituted for the scallops.

TACOS

WHEAT TORTILLAS

Wheat tortillas are more common in Northern Mexico and in the United States. They are generally larger and thinner than masa tortillas.

2 cups all-purpose flour (unbleached)
$\frac{1}{2}$ tsp. salt
$\frac{1}{2}$ tsp. baking powder, optional
2 tbs. canola or vegetable oil
$\frac{2}{3}$-$\frac{3}{4}$ cup water

Follow directions for making tortillas beginning on page 49. Makes 12 to 15 tortillas.

TIP: Wheat tortillas may be pressed several times in an electric tortilla press so that they become very thin. Turn tortillas frequently during baking. Do not press down on any bubbles as they form, as that helps form the layers in the tortillas.

TACOS

MASA TRIGO TORTILLAS

Masa trigo is a wheat flour that has been milled from lime-soaked wheat, in a similar method to masa harina. Masa trigo is available in Mexican groceries or mail order catalogs. This rolls or presses much like a basic wheat tortilla.

2 cups masa trigo
$\frac{1}{2}$ tsp. salt
$\frac{1}{2}$ tsp. baking powder, optional
1 tbs. canola or vegetable oil
$\frac{1}{2}$-$\frac{2}{3}$ cup water

Follow directions for making tortillas beginning on page 49. Makes 12 tortillas.

TACOS

MASA WHEAT TORTILLAS

Many people associate the lime-soaked corn flavor of masa harina with tortillas, but seem to prefer the flexibility of wheat tortillas for rolling. This nontraditional compromise between the two gives the best of both.

1 cup all-purpose flour (unbleached)
1 cup masa harina
½ tsp. salt
½ tsp. baking powder, optional
2 tbs. canola or vegetable oil
about ¾ cup water

Mix flour, masa harina, salt, baking powder and oil, adding water while mixing until a soft, workable dough is obtained. It is not necessary to form dough into balls to rest prior to making tortillas, as you do with plain corn masa tortillas. Follow remaining directions for making tortillas beginning on page 49. Makes 12 to 15 tortillas.

TACOS

SHRIMP FAJITAS

Fillings for fajitas are traditionally grilled with lemon or lime juice or tequila as a seasoning and are wrapped in warm, soft tortillas as a soft taco. This is an easy, nongrilled variation.

1 lb. shrimp, cleaned
1 tbs. olive oil
1 tbs. lemon juice
1 tbs. soy sauce
¼ medium onion, sliced
2 bell peppers, sliced

1 clove garlic, minced or pressed
1-2 jalapeño peppers, diced, or to taste
1 tsp. cumin, or 1 tbs. chile powder
¼ cup chopped fresh cilantro leaves, or
 to taste
salt and pepper to taste

In a large skillet, sauté shrimp in olive oil until they just begin to turn pink. Add remaining ingredients and cook until vegetables are tender-crisp. Serve immediately wrapped in warm tortillas. Makes 4 to 6 servings.

TACOS

CORNMEAL TORTILLAS

This recipe makes wonderful corn-flavored tortillas when you don't have any corn masa on hand.

1 cup water
1 cup cornmeal
2 cups all-purpose flour, unbleached
½ tsp. salt, optional
1 tsp. baking powder
1 tbs. canola or vegetable oil
¼-⅓ cup water, if and as necessary

Bring water to a boil, add cornmeal, remove from heat and soak cornmeal for 10 to 15 minutes. Add flour, salt, baking powder and oil and mix ingredients until well blended. Let mixture rest for about 30 minutes. Form dough into 12 to 15 balls and flatten them between the palms of your hands. Place these in a plastic bag to rest for 30 more minutes. Press in a tortilla press and cook, following directions for making tortillas beginning at Step 6, on page 50. Makes 12 to 15 tortillas.

TACOS

SHRIMP SALSA

This flavorful salsa may be served wrapped in a soft tortilla. We tested this by both spooning the salsa on top (my preference) and by heating it with the shrimp (testers' preference).

1-2 tbs. olive oil
1 lb. shrimp, cleaned
1 medium green bell pepper, chopped
¼ red onion, chopped
1-2 cloves garlic, minced
¼-½ cup salsa
fresh cilantro, salt and pepper to taste

Heat olive oil in a large skillet. Sauté shrimp, pepper, onion and garlic until shrimp is pink and vegetables are just soft. Add salsa and seasoning and simmer over very low heat for 5 minutes. Wrap in a warm tortilla. Makes 4 to 5 servings.

TIP: The shrimp is easier to eat if cut into bite-sized pieces. For a quick meal, add precooked shrimp to pepper and onions just as they finish cooking.

ENCHILADAS

Enchiladas are made with either softened corn or wheat (I prefer wheat) tortillas in which a filling of meat, cheese and/or vegetables is wrapped. The enchiladas are covered with a sauce and usually a cheese and baked. Traditional Mexican enchiladas are filled with shredded chicken, beef or beans and a tomato or picante sauce is used. There is no reason, however, why an Indian chicken curry may not be served in the same manner!

BASIC ENCHILADA DIRECTIONS

Use fresh, soft tortillas straight from the griddle or press, or soften a stack of 4 to 5 tortillas by warming between damp paper towels in a microwave for 1 to 2 minutes. Fill each tortilla with ¼ to ⅓ cup filling ingredients. Fold tortilla so that filling is encased and place seam side down in a lightly greased 9-x-13-inch baking dish. Repeat process until all tortillas and fillings are gone and dish is full. Pour sauce over enchiladas, sprinkle with cheese and any herbs if desired, and bake, uncovered, in a preheated 350° oven for 10 to 15 minutes.

ENCHILADAS

HOT AND SPICY TORTILLAS

These tortillas are so flavorful, you want to use them with a basic, not-too-spicy filling. They complement simple cheese enchiladas perfectly.

2 cups all-purpose flour (unbleached)
½ tsp. salt
¼-½ tsp. cayenne pepper
½ tsp. baking powder, optional
1-2 jalapeños, finely chopped
2 tbs. canola or vegetable oil
½-⅔ cup water

Follow directions for making tortillas beginning on page 49. Makes 12 to 15 tortillas.

ENCHILADAS

CHEESE ENCHILADAS

*Use this filling with any spicy tortilla such as **Hot and Spicy Tortillas**, page 70, or **Three Pepper Tortillas**, page 85.*

FILLING

1 lb. grated sharp cheddar or Colby cheese
1 medium onion, chopped or sliced

SAUCE

1 cup salsa or chili sauce

TOPPING

1/2 cup (2 oz.) grated cheese
chopped fresh herbs

To assemble and cook, follow *Basic Enchilada Directions*, page 69. Makes enough for 12 to 15 tortillas.

ENCHILADAS

TRADITIONAL MEXICAN ENCHILADAS

*These enchiladas are wonderful with either the basic **Wheat Tortillas**, page 63, or the **Cilantro Tortillas**, page 61.*

SAUCE

¼-½ medium red onion, preferably Bermuda
1-2 cloves garlic
1-2 jalapeño peppers, or to taste
1 can (14.5 oz.) whole tomatoes, drained, or about 6 fresh, Roma (Italian) tomatoes
¼ cup fresh cilantro leaves
salt and pepper to taste

Using a food processor or blender, process onions, garlic and peppers until finely chopped. Add remaining ingredients and process until tomatoes are just chopped and ingredients are blended.

ENCHILADAS

FILLING

1 lb. cooked, shredded or diced chicken, or 1 lb. cooked ground beef,
  taco-seasoned (see page 57)
cooked onion slices, optional

TOPPING

about 1 cup (4 oz.) grated cheddar cheese

To assemble and cook, follow *Basic Enchilada Directions*, page 69. Makes enough for 12 to 15 tortillas.

ENCHILADAS

INDIAN ENCHILADAS

*Who said that enchiladas were limited to just Mexican style? Use the basic **Wheat Tortillas** recipe, page 63, so you don't overwhelm the filling.*

SAUCE

1 can (14.5 oz.) chopped tomatoes
¼ tsp. dried red pepper flakes, or to taste
2 tbs.-¼ cup chopped onion
½ small zucchini, grated
2 cloves garlic, minced or pressed
½ tsp. cumin
¼ tsp. coriander seed
1 tsp. curry
1 tbs. freshly chopped ginger root, or 1 tsp. ground ginger
salt and pepper to taste

In a large saucepan, mix together sauce ingredients and simmer over low heat for about 5 minutes.

ENCHILADAS

FILLING

1-2 tbs. olive oil
1 lb. cooked shrimp, or 3 cooked, boneless chicken breasts, diced
1 medium bell pepper, diced
½ medium red onion, diced
cilantro or parsley to taste
salt and pepper to taste

TOPPING

¼-½ cup plain nonfat yogurt

To assemble and cook, follow *Basic Enchilada Directions*, page 69. Makes enough for 12 to 15 tortillas.

TOSTADAS

Tostadas are tortillas that are cooked or lightly fried until golden brown and crisp and are then layered with various foods.

BASIC TOSTADA DIRECTIONS

If making fresh tortillas, simply cook each side longer on the ungreased griddle so that the tortilla is just getting hard and crispy (low fat version). If using already made tortillas, you may either cook them on an ungreased griddle, fry lightly in an inch of canola oil or lard, or bake in a 400° oven until crisp. Drain on a paper towel. In order, layer the tostada with beans, meat, lettuce, tomatoes, cheese, guacamole and sour cream, or use any combination that pleases you.

TOSTADAS

TOMATO TORTILLAS

The tomato gives the tortillas both a nice flavor and an attractive color that blend especially well with black beans.

1 cup masa harina
1 cup all-purpose flour
½ tsp. baking powder
½ tsp. salt, optional
1 tbs. canola or vegetable oil
⅔ cup tomato juice (5.5 oz. can)
¼-⅓ cup water

Follow directions for making tortillas beginning on page 49. Makes 12 to 15 tortillas.

TOSTADAS

BLACK BEAN TOSTADAS

*This tostada topping combines nicely with **Tomato Tortillas,** page 77. Use canned beans for convenience, but rinse thoroughly to remove excess salt.*

1/2-3/4 cup salsa
1 can (16 oz.) black beans, rinsed and drained
1/2 medium red onion, chopped or sliced
jalapeño peppers, chopped or sliced, to taste
dried red pepper flakes to taste, optional
cilantro to taste, optional
1 cup grated Monterey Jack cheese (4 oz.)
1 cup grated cheddar cheese (4 oz.)
salsa and sour cream for topping

In a large skillet, heat salsa, black beans and onion until onion is golden. Season to taste with peppers and cilantro. Simmer over low heat for 3 to 5 minutes or until just warmed. Place filling on crisp or fried tortillas and top with cheeses, more salsa and/or sour cream. Makes 3 to 3 1/2 cups.

TIP: Use this as a filling for tacos or burritos.

TOSTADAS

TORTILLA PIZZA

Tortilla pizzas may be found in many restaurants these days, but they are really a variation of a tostada. Use only mozzarella or a combination of mozzarella, Monterey Jack and cheddar cheese. The given amounts are approximations only — use amounts to your taste, but do not overload.

2-3 tbs. salsa
scant ¼ cup black beans, or taco-seasoned ground meat
1 tbs. finely chopped onions or peppers
¼ cup grated cheese (1 oz.)

Crisp tortilla according to tostada directions on page 76. Spread a small amount of salsa on top of crisped tortilla. Layer remaining ingredients (or those of your choice) and place under a broiler just long enough to melt cheese.

QUESADILLAS

Quesadillas are tortillas which are lightly fried with the cheese and/or other filling ingredients on top or inside.

BASIC QUESADILLA DIRECTIONS

FOLDED QUESADILLAS: Use an uncooked tortilla dough that has been rolled or pressed. Spoon 2 to 3 tbs. cheese or filling ingredients onto one half of the dough. Fold the other half over the top and seal shut by pressing the edges closed with your fingers. Fry for 1 minute on each side in 1/2 to 1 inch hot canola oil or lard. Serve hot.

FLAT QUESADILLAS: Layer cheese and any other ingredients on top of a flour tortilla. Place on a hot, ungreased griddle and cook for 3 to 5 minutes until the cheese has melted and the tortilla is just beginning to crisp. Top the filling with another tortilla and flip over to grill the other side for a "sandwich" quesadilla.

Quesadillas are like tacos in that everyone makes his or her own by adding ingredients of choice in varying amounts. I generally use a combination of cheddar and Monterey Jack cheese and place only enough cheese so that they will not overflow. I like to add fresh, chopped tomatoes along with a variety of diced vegetables (green bell peppers, snow peas, scallions, cilantro etc.). Some people like to add cooked meats (crab, shrimp, chicken, etc.)

QUESADILLAS

BLUE CORN TORTILLAS

Blue corn is native to the American Southwest and has a wonderful, nutty flavor.

¾ cup blue cornmeal
2 cups all-purpose flour (unbleached)
½ tsp. salt, optional
1 tsp. baking powder
1 tbs. canola or vegetable oil
¾-⅞ cup warm water

Follow directions for making tortillas beginning on page 49. Makes 12 to 15 tortillas.

QUESADILLAS

BASIC OR SPICY QUESADILLA FILLING

*The cayenne pepper turns the cheese filling bright red, and makes a colorful quesadilla. Use this with basic tortillas such as **Blue Corn Tortillas**, page 81.*

1 cup ricotta cheese
½ cup grated Monterey Jack cheese
1 egg
½ tsp. cayenne pepper, optional for spicy version
2-3 finely chopped jalapeño peppers, optional for spicy version

Mix ingredients together and fill each quesadilla with 2 to 3 tbs. filling. Makes enough filling for 6 to 8 quesadillas.

TIP: This basic cheese filling may be varied according to your taste. The cayenne and jalapeños may be omitted and replaced with either chopped onions and/or fresh herbs, or you may simply use the two cheeses and egg so you won't overwhelm any other portion of your meal.

QUESADILLAS

BLACK BEAN TORTILLAS

Black bean tortillas combine nicely with just about any filling, especially with cheddar cheese and onions!

1 can black beans
2 cups masa harina
½ tsp. salt, optional
1 tsp. baking powder
½ tsp. onion powder
1 tbs. canola or vegetable oil
1¼-1⅓ cups warm water

Black beans must be well rinsed and drained and then processed in a blender or food processor until pureed. A tablespoon or two of water may be added to assist in obtaining a smooth texture. Add dry ingredients and mix well. Add oil. Add water slowly as you continue to mix ingredients to the proper consistency. Knead until smooth, about 2 minutes. Follow directions for making tortillas beginning with Step 2 on page 49. Makes 12 to 15 tortillas.

QUESADILLAS

ONION QUESADILLAS

Crunchy onions combined with a sharp cheddar cheese make a great quesadilla filling when paired with black bean tortillas.

1 medium onion, sliced
½ lb. sharp cheddar cheese, grated
2 large tomatoes, seeded and diced
¼ cup fresh cilantro leaves

Either layer ingredients on tortillas prior to cooking, or mix all ingredients together and fill quesadillas with a heaping tablespoon of mixture. Fills about 12 quesadillas.

QUESADILLAS

THREE PEPPER TORTILLAS

This blend of three peppers is a favorite of mine whether in pasta, pizza or tortillas. It complements just about any food used for topping or filling.

2 cups all-purpose flour (unbleached)
1/2 tsp. salt
1 tsp. coarsely ground black pepper
1/2 tsp. cayenne pepper

1/2 tsp. white pepper
1/2 tsp. baking powder, optional
2 tbs. canola or vegetable oil
2/3-3/4 cup water

Follow directions for making tortillas beginning on page 49. Makes 12 to 15.

HERBED QUESADILLA FILLING

This blend of cheeses goes well with any hot and/or flavorful tortilla. I like to use cilantro, but basil or parsley may also be used.

1 cup ricotta cheese
1/2 cup grated Monterey Jack cheese
1/4-1/3 cup chopped fresh herbs

1 egg
1/2 tsp. salt

Combine ingredients, blending well. Fills 12 to 15 quesadillas.

BURRITOS

Burritos are flour tortillas folded around a warm, traditional filling of beans, held in the hand and eaten. Burritos that are fried are called chimichangas (fry in an inch or so of oil in a large skillet, or deep fry).

BASIC BURRITO DIRECTIONS

Use a freshly made or warm tortilla. Place about ¼ cup filling ingredients vertically down the center of the upper ¾ of the tortilla. Fold the bottom of the tortilla up over the filling and then each side up and over so that the filling is tightly encased on three sides.

BURRITO FILLINGS

Any tortilla may be used. Basically, any filling that may be used in a taco, may be used in a burrito. Egg fillings seem to blend with the nutty flavor of the amaranth when using amaranth tortillas. See *Taco Buffet*, page 56.

For breakfast, fill the burrito with scrambled eggs and chorizo (or any sausage), or scrambled eggs with salsa and onion. For other meals during the day, use taco meat and cheese, or refried beans seasoned with garlic, cumin, salt and pepper, and sprinkled with cheese.

BURRITOS

AMARANTH TORTILLAS

Although amaranth is indigenous to Mexico, there is little information to be found about amaranth tortillas. The only mention discovered in my research dealt with the Aztecs mixing human blood with amaranth to form edible cakes. This is one reason the Spanish conquistadors burned all known fields of amaranth! Suffice it to say that this recipe uses water....

½ cup amaranth flour
2 cups all-purpose flour (unbleached)
½ tsp. salt
1 tsp. baking powder
2 tbs. canola or vegetable oil
1 tbs. honey
about ¾ cup warm water

Follow directions for making tortillas beginning on page 49. Makes 12 to 15 tortillas.

BURRITOS

BREAKFAST BURRITO

If you want a fiery start to your day, try this for breakfast! It is also good any other time of the day. Adjust the ingredients (amounts and types) to suit your mood or to use what you have in the refrigerator.

½ tbs. canola or vegetable oil
2 tbs. finely chopped onion
½ bell pepper, chopped (any color)
4 eggs
salt to taste (about ¼-½ tsp.)
½ tsp. pepper
¼ cup grated cheddar cheese
½ cup salsa

Heat oil in a large skillet and cook onion and bell pepper until they just begin to soften. Do not overcook. Meanwhile, beat together eggs, seasonings and cheese. Pour egg mixture into skillet and cook, stirring frequently, until scrambled eggs set. Stir in salsa and warm on low heat for a minute or two. Serve wrapped in a warm tortilla. Makes about 6 servings.

BURRITOS

SWEET TORTILLAS

Great for breakfast! The walnut oil adds a special, nutty flavor. If you cannot locate walnut oil in your grocery store, any other nut or vegetable oil may be substituted. My children eat these with butter and cinnamon sugar for breakfast. Or, try rolling raisins, chopped nuts, melted butter and cinnamon sugar inside for a "raisin bun."

2 cups all-purpose flour (unbleached)
½ tsp. salt
1 tbs. sugar
1 tsp. cinnamon
½ tsp. baking powder, optional
2 tbs. walnut oil
⅔-¾ cup water

Follow directions for making tortillas beginning on page 49. Makes 12 to 15 tortillas.

BURRITOS

ORANGE CHICKEN

*Serve this flavorful fruit chicken (or turkey) wrapped in a **Sweet Tortilla**, page 89, for any meal of the day! For lunch or a light dinner, serve with a tossed green salad.*

2 tbs. orange juice
½ tsp. salt
½ tsp. pepper
1 tsp. cinnamon, or to taste
dash fresh nutmeg
1 lb. ground chicken or turkey
¼ cup sliced or chopped almonds
1 can (10 oz.) mandarin orange segments, drained

Mix together juice, salt, pepper, cinnamon and nutmeg. Add ground meat and mix well. Cook immediately or refrigerate for 1 to several hours. In a large skillet, cook meat until done (no oil is needed). When meat is done, add nuts and well-drained orange segments and heat over low heat until just warmed. Serve warm wrapped in a tortilla. Makes 2 to 2½ cups.

BAKED FLATBREADS

PITA OR ARABIAN BREAD

Even though pita breads are leavened with yeast (or sourdough in some cases), they are considered a flatbread because they are used as "edible plates." Pitas have become popular, served in many sandwich shops with every type of filling imaginable.

3 cups all-purpose flour
2 tsp. dry yeast (active or rapid)
1 tbs. sugar
1/2 tsp. salt

1 1/8 cups lukewarm water
1 tbs. olive oil
additional olive oil for brushing, optional

Make yeast dough following directions on page 6. Allow dough to rise for about 1 hour after kneading. Punch down dough and divide it into 6 to 8 pieces. Flatten each piece by hand, with a rolling pin or a nonelectric tortilla press, into a small circle, about 6 inches in diameter. Fold each side of circle in towards the center and then roll out again to a 6-inch circle. Sprinkle each circle very lightly with water (I do this with wet fingers), cover with a kitchen towel and let rise for about 30 minutes. Brush top with a little olive oil (optional). For best puffing results, place pitas on a preheated baking sheet or perforated pizza pan and bake in a preheated 500° oven for 7 to 8 minutes. Wrap pitas in a clean kitchen towel immediately after removing from oven or place them in a brown paper bag to cool to prevent crisping. Makes 6 to 8.

PITA OR ARABIAN BREAD

TIP: The pita rounds may simply be rolled into a circle and left to rise, but I have had much better success with the "pockets" forming when I roll the circles twice as described. If pockets do not form, fold the ingredients inside or cut a pocket.

GREEK SHRIMP

This is quick and easy light fare when stuffed inside a pita pocket. Measurements for filling ingredients need not be exact but are adjusted to taste.

4 oz. crumbled feta cheese
1 green onion, white and green part, chopped

1 lb. cooked shrimp, peeled and finely chopped
salt and pepper to taste
Yogurt Sauce, follows

Fill pita pocket with feta, onion, shrimp and seasoning. Top with yogurt sauce. Makes 4 to 5 servings.

YOGURT SAUCE

1 cup plain nonfat yogurt
1/4 cup chopped fresh parsley, or mint

1 clove garlic, minced
1/2 tsp. pepper

Process ingredients with a food processor until well blended. Refrigerate for at least 1 hour. Makes about 1 cup.

HERBED PITA

One of the all-time joys of making your own breads is the ability to flavor and color the breads to complement any filling. Any herb (basil, mint, cilantro, parsley, etc.) may replace the oregano, but the oregano enhances the flavor of the gyro filling.

3-3¼ cups all-purpose flour
2 tsp. dry yeast (active or rapid)
1 tbs. sugar
½ tsp. salt
1 tsp. coarsely ground black pepper
1 tsp. minced garlic
1 tbs. fresh oregano, or 1 tsp. dried
1⅛ cups lukewarm water
1 tbs. olive oil

Follow general directions for yeast breads, page 6, and *Pita*, page 92. Makes 6 to 8.

HERBED PITA

GYRO

Gyros are one of my all-time favorite sandwiches. The meat that is used is a combination of ground lamb and beef which is pressed and cut into thin strips. As this meat is not something you can usually buy in the grocery stores, I use a combination of ground lamb and ground beef.

½ lb. ground beef
½ lb. ground lamb
1 tbs. chopped fresh oregano, or 1 tsp. dried
1 tsp. minced garlic
salt and pepper to taste
Tzatziki Sauce, page 96
slices of raw white onion
fresh parsley, optional

Combine all ingredients and cook immediately or place in the refrigerator for 1 to several hours. Cook in a large skillet until meat is no longer pink. Drain well. Serve wrapped in a pita with *Tzatziki Sauce* and slices of onion and fresh parsley, if desired. Makes 2 cups.

HERBED PITA

TZATZIKI (SATZIKI) SAUCE

This cucumber yogurt sauce is spooned liberally on top of the gyro. It also may be served as a side to any lamb dish.

1 cup plain nonfat or low fat yogurt, made without gelatin
$\frac{1}{2}$ tsp. salt
1 cup finely chopped cucumber (about 1 medium)
1 tsp. minced garlic
$\frac{1}{2}$ tsp. white pepper
dash sugar
1 tsp. white wine vinegar
1 tbs. olive oil

Place yogurt in a small colander lined with several layers of cheesecloth or coffee filters. Place colander over a small bowl into which whey will drain. Place colander and bowl in the refrigerator for approximately 2 hours. Discard whey. Combine thickened yogurt (yogurt "cheese") with remaining ingredients and refrigerate for several hours. Makes about 1 to 1$\frac{1}{2}$ cups.

TIP: Yogurt cheese makers are available in some gourmet stores.

HERBED PITA

PAKISTANI LAMB

Somehow lamb and pitas go hand in hand. I use ground lamb for convenience.

MARINADE

1/4 cup almonds
1/4 cup olive oil
1 tbs. white vinegar
1 tbs. lemon juice
1-2 cloves garlic
1/4 medium red onion
1/2 tsp. cinnamon
1/8 tsp. cardamom

1/8 tsp. coriander
1 tsp. cumin
1 tsp. sugar
1/2 tsp. salt
1 tsp. coarsely ground black pepper
1/4 tsp. dried mint, or 2 fresh mint leaves
1/2 tsp. dried cilantro, or leaves from 1
 stalk

1 lb. ground lamb   *Yogurt Topping*, page 98

Process almonds in a food processor until very finely ground. Add all remaining marinade ingredients and process until well blended. Pour over lamb in a glass or plastic bowl, cover and refrigerate for several hours. In a large skillet, cook lamb in marinade until it is no longer pink. Drain. Serve wrapped in a soft pita or in the pocket of a pita, topped with *Yogurt Topping*. Makes 2 to 2 1/2 cups.

HERBED PITA

YOGURT TOPPING

1 cup plain nonfat yogurt
1/4 cup fresh cilantro leaves
salt and pepper to taste

In the workbowl of a food processor or in a blender, process ingredients together until cilantro is very finely chopped and blended with yogurt. Refrigerate until ready to serve. Makes about 1 cup.

TIP: If you want to make kabobs, marinate 2-inch cubes of boneless leg of lamb in the marinade for 6 to 8 hours. Place meat on skewers and grill until done. Serve with *Yogurt Topping*.

BARBARI

These basic breads of Persian origin are scored to prevent pockets from forming. Use pieces of the bread to scoop up foods or to soak up sauces.

2 cups all-purpose flour
1½ tsp. dry yeast (active or rapid)
1 tsp. salt
1 tbs. olive oil

¾ cup warm water
additional olive oil for brushing
  and rolling

Make a stiff yeast dough according to directions on page 6. Form dough into 2 or 3 equal balls. Brush each ball lightly with olive oil and roll on a lightly oiled (instead of floured) work surface to prevent sticking. Shape each ball into a large circle or rectangle about ½- to ¾-inch thick. Place dough on a lightly greased baking sheet, cover with a towel and let rise in a warm, draft-free location for 20 to 30 minutes. Brush top of dough with olive oil. Using a sharp knife or razor blade, cut 4 or 5 parallel lines running the length of the bread. If making a rectangular loaf, make cuts going in the opposite direction as well, forming small squares. Bake in a preheated 425° oven for approximately 15 minutes. Cut into small sections for serving. Makes 2 or 3 rounds.

TIP: After brushing with oil and cutting the grooves, vary by sprinkling with seeds such as sesame, anise, fennel, caraway, etc.

BARBARI

LAMB KABOBS

*Kabobs are generally eaten with rice, stuffed into pita pockets or eaten with breads such as **Barbari**. Mahlab is a flavoring made from ground black cherry pits which is often used in Middle Eastern cooking. It may be purchased from mail order sources or some specialty shops in seed form and must be cracked with a mortar and pestle. Allspice or cinnamon may be used as a substitute for mahlab.*

MARINADE

⅓ cup olive oil
¼ cup red wine, or red wine vinegar
½ tsp. salt

1 tsp. coarsely ground black pepper
1 tsp. ground mahlab

---

1 lb. leg of lamb, cut into 2-3-inch cubes   quartered onion with pieces separated

Mix together marinade ingredients. Toss with lamb cubes and refrigerate for 6 to 8 hours. Remove meat from marinade and place on skewers alternately with onion slices. Grill over medium to high heat until meat is only slightly pink in the middle. Serve with a spaghetti sauce or a yogurt sauce (see pages 93 or 98) as a topping. Makes 4 to 5 servings.

TALAMI

This Lebanese flatbread may be used to wrap around food or to pick up any remaining sauces from plates. This is similar to a pita bread, but it includes egg for a little extra richness and flavor.

3 cups all-purpose flour
1½ tsp. dry yeast (active or rapid)
1 tbs. sugar
1 tsp. salt
1 egg
2 tbs. vegetable oil
1 cup water

Prepare yeast dough according to directions on page 6. Allow dough to rise following kneading for 30 to 40 minutes. Form dough into 8 or 9 equal balls. On a floured work surface, roll into 6- or 7-inch circles. Place on a greased baking sheet, cover and let rest for about 10 minutes. Press surface of dough just before baking (to prevent a pocket from forming) and bake in a preheated 450° oven for 7 to 8 minutes until lightly brown. Makes 8 or 9.

TALAMI

MIDDLE EASTERN LAMB

*This versatile filling may be used in pita pockets or wrapped in **Talami**, empanadas or soft tortillas. The pine nuts may be used whole or chopped.*

1 lb. ground lamb
1/4 cup diced or sliced onion
1 clove garlic, minced
1 tbs. olive oil
salt and pepper to taste

1/2 tsp. cinnamon
1 tsp. dried basil, or 1 tbs. chopped fresh
1/4 cup pine nuts, or chopped walnuts
8 oz. crumbled feta cheese
1 cup plain yogurt (for pitas or tortillas)

In a large skillet, cook ground lamb, onion and garlic in olive oil. Season with salt, pepper, cinnamon and basil. Drain grease and crumble meat. Combine with pine nuts and feta. Fill bread and top with yogurt. Makes 2 cups.

NAAN (YEAST-LEAVENED)

Indian naan is similar to a pita bread, but is somewhat richer, as it is usually made with yogurt. Naan is traditionally baked in a tandoor, a brick oven.

2 cups all-purpose flour
1½ tsp. dry yeast (active or rapid)
1 tsp. sugar
½ tsp. salt
2 tbs. vegetable oil
¼ cup plain nonfat yogurt
about ½ cup water to adjust consistency of dough

Prepare yeast dough according to directions on page 6. Form dough into 5 or 6 balls and flatten each ball into a 6-inch circle or oval. Bake in a preheated 500° oven for 5 to 7 minutes. If you wish, you may brown by cooking each side briefly on a very hot, ungreased griddle after baking. Makes 5 or 6.

NAAN (YEAST-LEAVENED)

SIMPLE NAAN TOPPING

This topping goes best with the yeast-leavened, raised, oven-baked naan. Sometimes naan is served plain with a meal. At other times, the breads are eaten as a snack, either plain or topped with onions and sesame seeds.

1-2 tbs. olive oil
¼ cup onion slivers
1-2 tbs. sesame seeds

Lightly brush each naan with just enough oil to cover top of dough. Gently press onion slivers into dough and sprinkle top with sesame seeds. Bake in a preheated 500° oven for 5 to 7 minutes. Serve warm or cool.

NAAN (YEAST-LEAVENED)

SPICY CHICKEN

Yogurt is a staple food in India and is often seasoned and used as a marinade for many meats. This recipe is based on one which is usually served wrapped in a naan. If desired, chopped tomatoes and onions may be served as an additional topping.

MARINADE

2 cups plain nonfat yogurt
1 tsp. freshly grated ginger root, or
   ¼ tsp. ground ginger
1-2 jalapeño peppers, finely chopped

1-2 garlic cloves, minced or pressed
1 scallion, diced
½ tsp. salt
1 tsp. coarsely ground black pepper

1 lb. boneless chicken breasts (3 or 4)

Mix together marinade ingredients and pour over chicken in a glass or plastic container. Refrigerate for 1 to 4 hours. Grill chicken over medium-high heat until tender, basting with marinade as needed. Heat any remaining marinade in the microwave or in a small saucepan over low heat. Cut chicken into bite-sized pieces and place in middle of a naan. Spoon heated marinade on top and wrap to eat. Makes 4 to 5 servings.

TIP: For a quick and easy version of this recipe, use leftover cooked chicken or turkey. Pour marinade over meat and refrigerate for at least 1 hour. Warm chicken and marinade and serve as directed.

MIDDLE EASTERN (ARMENIAN) LAVASH

*While these may look like tortillas, they are generally much larger. These breads may be cooked for a short time for a soft, pliable bread, or longer for a crispy bread. The crisp flatbreads are served with butter or as an accompaniment to curried dishes. The softer version is often spread with fillings and rolled into sandwich rolls, or filled like soft tortillas with cheese, grilled meat or sometimes just fresh herbs. **Lavash** is usually served warm, either freshly made or warmed in the oven just before serving.*

1 tsp. salt
3 cups all-purpose flour
1-1⅛ cups warm water

Mix salt with flour and work in water until a soft, workable dough is obtained. Divide dough into 6 or 7 equal pieces and roll with a rolling pin into 10-inch paper-thin circles. Flour your work surface only if absolutely necessary to roll well. Bake in a preheated 400° oven for 3 to 4 minutes. Wrap cooked lavash in a kitchen towel to keep warm until serving. Makes 6 or 7.

MIDDLE EASTERN (ARMENIAN) LAVASH

CHICKEN CURRY

This is based on a Middle Eastern curry recipe.

1-2 tbs. curry powder
1 tsp. cinnamon
1 tbs. brown sugar
2 tbs. lime juice
2 tbs. lemon juice
¼ cup olive oil
¼ cup chopped fresh cilantro leaves
2 jalapeño or red peppers (or to taste), finely chopped
1 lb. boneless chicken breasts (3 or 4)

Mix together all ingredients except chicken, blending well. Pour over chicken in a glass or plastic container. Refrigerate for several hours. Grill chicken, basting with marinade as needed. Makes 4 to 5 servings.

TIP: Shrimp may be used instead of chicken. Cook shrimp in the marinade until pink.

MIDDLE EASTERN CRISPBREAD

Unlike pitas, these breads are flat and crisp. If you have a pizza stone, bake them directly on the stone for best results. Crispbreads may be used for appetizers or eaten with any Middle Eastern meal.

2 cups all-purpose flour
1½ tsp. fast-acting dry yeast
1 tsp. sugar
1 tsp. salt
3 tbs. olive oil
½ cup warm water

Make yeast dough following directions on page 6. After dough has risen, punch it down well. Divide dough in half and roll each half into a rectangle on a lightly floured work surface. Place each rectangle on a cornmeal-covered baking sheet or on a perforated pizza pan and bake in a preheated 450° oven for 12 to 18 minutes or until golden brown. Cool on wire racks. The longer the bread bakes, the crispier it becomes. Makes 2.

MIDDLE EASTERN CRISPBREAD

DUKKA

*This is based on an Egyptian recipe which is usually eaten with bread dipped in olive oil. I find it quite easy to use the **Middle Eastern Crispbread** recipe baked so that it is still soft (about 12 minutes) and spread with this delightful combination. I use a blend of red and black pepper which I buy in the grocery store. Any leftovers may be kept for several weeks in the refrigerator.*

olive oil to coat skillet
1/2 cup sesame seeds
2 tbs. anise, coriander or cumin seeds

1/2 tsp. coarse salt
1/2 tsp. red or black pepper
olive oil to spread on bread

Using a paper towel, rub a very small amount of olive oil on the bottom of a medium-sized, heavy (cast iron) skillet. Heat until the pan is hot and then lower the temperature. Toast all seeds until they just begin to brown — only a minute or two — do not overcook. Place all ingredients in a food processor and process, using the steel blade, until seeds are finely crushed.

Spread olive oil on top of cooked bread and sprinkle seeds on top to serve. Or, serve bread alone (crisp or soft) with olive oil and dukka in individual bowls. To eat, dip each bite of bread into oil and then into seeds. Makes 2/3 cup.

FLAVORED MIDDLE EASTERN CRISPBREAD

This herb-flavored flatbread may be served as an accompaniment to a meal or as a snack by itself. Any fresh herb may be used to complement a meal. Try basil, mint, parsley or cilantro.

2 cups all-purpose flour
1½ tsp. fast-acting dry yeast (active or rapid)
1 tsp. sugar
½ tsp. salt
2 tbs. chopped fresh herbs
¼ cup chopped onion
1-2 tsp. chopped roasted red peppers (sold in jars)
2 tbs. olive oil
about ½ cup warm water

Make yeast dough following directions on page 6. After dough has risen, punch it down well. Divide dough in half and roll each half into a rectangle on a lightly floured counter. Place each rectangle on a cornmeal-covered baking sheet or a perforated pizza pan and bake in a preheated 450° oven for 12 to 20 minutes or until golden brown. Cool on wire racks. Makes 2.

FLAVORED MIDDLE EASTERN CRISPBREAD

CRISPBREAD APPETIZERS

It is traditional to serve fresh herbs and cheese with bread either before or after a meal. This extremely easy, low fat, herbed cheese is great spread over flavored crispbread and served for appetizers. Use the same herb as you use in the bread itself. The yogurt gives the topping a tangy flavor. Cream cheese may be substituted.

1 cup yogurt cheese
1 tsp. minced garlic

¼ cup chopped fresh herbs
1 tsp. coarsely ground black pepper

To make yogurt cheese, use nonfat, plain yogurt without gelatin added. Line a small colander with several thickness of coffee filter and place it over a small bowl so that the whey will drip into the bowl. Place yogurt in colander and refrigerate for several hours. Measure yogurt after it becomes "cheese."

Mix all ingredients until well blended. Spread on flavored crispbread and serve as appetizers.

TIP: If the bread is cooked a shorter time so that it is softer (about 12 minutes), the herbed cheese filling may be spread on the bread, rolled in a jelly-roll fashion and cut into pinwheels for serving. Slices of meats and/or cheeses may be added to the herb cheese blend or in place of it.

FLATBREADS AS PLATES

ITALIAN THIN CRUST PIZZA

A book on flatbreads cannot exist without mentioning pizza. Pizza has almost become the definition of "flatbread" — a grain-based bread dough upon which toppings are placed, baked and eaten. This is a basic pizza dough recipe for a single 15-inch thin crust. For many pizza dough and topping recipes, see my recent book, The Best Pizza Is Made At Home.

3 cups all-purpose flour
1½ tsp. dry yeast (active or rapid)
¼-½ tsp. salt
½ tsp. sugar, optional
1 tbs. olive or vegetable oil
1 cup warm water

Prepare yeast dough according to directions on page 6. Roll dough into a large, thin circle or rectangle and place on a greased pizza pan or baking sheet. Cover with toppings and bake in a preheated 500° oven until golden brown, about 5 to 10 minutes.

ITALIAN THIN CRUST PIZZA

PIZZA SAUCE

There are many bottled pizza sauces available in grocery and gourmet stores which may be perfectly acceptable. It is also easy to make your own sauce.

6-8 fresh Italian plum tomatoes
1-2 tsp. minced garlic
2 tbs. chopped fresh oregano, or 2 tsp. dried

1 tbs. chopped fresh basil, or 1 tsp. dried
salt to taste
red and/or black pepper to taste

Seed tomatoes by cutting off stem top and squeezing over a bowl or sink to remove seeds and excess juice. Process tomatoes in a blender or food processor for just a moment to chop coarsely. Add herbs and seasonings to taste. This may be used immediately, or if it will be refrigerated, simmer over low heat for 5 to 10 minutes. Allow to cool before placing in a tightly sealed container. Makes about 1 cup.

PIZZA TOPPINGS

Use about 2 cups (8 oz.) grated mozzarella cheese. Provolone and/or Parmesan may be used to replace as much as half the mozzarella.

Cooked meats, poultry, seafood, vegetables and even fruits may be added to the top of pizza in whatever combination you desire. Overloading the pizza with cheese and toppings results in a soggy crust which is difficult to handle.

FOCACCIA

This cousin to pizza is traditionally topped with olive oil, fresh basil or rosemary and coarse salt. This recipe flavors the dough too, for an undeniable winner.

3 cups all-purpose flour
1½ tsp. dry yeast (active or rapid)
½ tsp. salt
1 tsp. sugar
2 tbs. chopped fresh basil or rosemary, or 2 tsp. dried
2 tsp. minced garlic
¼ cup olive oil
1 cup lukewarm water

Make yeast dough according to directions on page 6. After allowing dough to rest for 1 hour, punch down and shape into a 9- or 10-inch round. Place in a deep dish pizza pan or on a baking sheet, cover and let rise in a warm, draft-free location for 30 to 40 minutes. Cover with toppings and bake in a preheated 400° oven for 25 to 30 minutes.

FOCACCIA

FOCACCIA TOPPING

While I have given you a fairly traditional topping, please use whatever similar toppings you would like to complement your meal. Dried herbs just don't cut it on a focaccia!

PER FOCACCIA:

2 tbs. olive oil
2-3 cloves of garlic, slivered
 AND/OR ¼ onion, finely slivered
1 tbs. freshly chopped herbs, or to taste
coarse salt to taste

After dough has risen, brush it all over with olive oil. Press garlic and/or onion slivers into dough with your fingers. This will also form small indentations in the dough. Lightly press fresh herbs into dough and sprinkle top with coarse salt. Bake in a preheated 400° oven for 25 to 30 minutes.

KHACHAPURI

This Georgian "pizza" dough is traditionally oval-shaped and is topped with anything from goat cheese to meat to beans.

3 cups all-purpose flour
1½ tsp. dry yeast
dash salt
1 tsp. sugar
2 tbs. vegetable oil
1-1⅛ cups water

After dough has risen, divide into 4 equal pieces and roll each into an oval shape. Place each oval on a lightly greased pizza pan or baking sheet, cover and let rise for about 15 minutes. Top with either of the two following toppings and bake in a preheated 500° oven for 8 to 10 minutes. Makes 4.

KHACHAPURI

KHACHAPURI CHEESE TOPPING

If goat cheese is too strong for you, try blending farmers cheese with it. The tomato is not traditional but always seems to blend with goat cheese! Fresh basil or cilantro may be added.

6 oz. goat cheese (chevré), crumbled
  OR 3 oz. each goat cheese and farmers cheese
tomato slices
2 slices of bacon, cooked and broken into bite-sized pieces for garnish

Leaving a ½- to 1-inch border (turned up to keep in cheese) on each oval piece of dough, top with cheese, a few tomato slices and bacon. Bake in a preheated 500° oven for 8 to 10 minutes or until bubbly and a light golden color. Makes enough for 4.

KHACHAPURI

BEAN TOPPING

Beans are often combined with a grain such as corn or wheat because it tastes good and because the combination produces complete protein, important for good nutrition. This is a variation of a Georgian bean-filled pastry dish.

1 can (15¼ oz.) kidney or black beans
1-2 tbs. olive oil
½-1 medium red onion, finely chopped
½ cup cilantro leaves, or to taste
salt to taste
black and/or red pepper to taste
1 cup grated cheddar cheese (4 oz.)

Rinse and drain beans. In a large skillet, heat olive oil and sauté onion until golden, stirring occasionally. Set aside to cool. Mash beans in a food processor with cilantro. Add onion, salt and pepper and process briefly until just blended. Divide topping and spread on top of khachapuri dough. Top with cheddar cheese and bake in a preheated 500° oven for 8 to 10 minutes. Makes 4 servings.

ARABIAN PIZZA

These small pizzas make great snacks or appetizers. The crust is thick and is soft enough to fold for easier eating, if desired.

3 cups all-purpose flour
2 tsp. dry yeast (active or rapid)
1 tsp. salt
½ tsp. sugar
3 tbs. olive oil
¾-1 cup lukewarm water

Make yeast dough according to directions on page 6. Allow dough to rise for 2 hours after kneading.

Punch dough down and divide into 6 or 7 pieces. Roll each piece into a small circle (about 6 inches in diameter). Spread ⅓ to ½ cup topping over dough and transfer to a greased baking sheet. Bake in a preheated 450° oven for about 7 minutes or until light brown and still soft. Makes 6 or 7.

ARABIAN PIZZA

CHEESE PIZZA TOPPING

Greek feta cheese gives this a real Middle Eastern flavor which blends with the dough. Cooked ground lamb and onions may be added on top as a variation. The lamb is optional — the cheese topping alone makes a great pizza.

1 egg
1 cup ricotta cheese
3/4 cup freshly grated Parmesan cheese
2 oz. crumbled feta cheese (1/2 cup)

1/4 cup chopped fresh parsley, or
 1 tbs. dried
1 green onion, finely chopped
salt and pepper to taste

1/4-1/2 medium onion, diced, optional
1 lb. cooked ground lamb, optional

olive oil for cooking
ground cinnamon, optional

Mix egg into ricotta cheese. Add cheeses, parsley, green onion, salt and pepper and mix until just blended. This cheese mixture may be refrigerated until needed.

In a large skillet, cook onion and ground lamb in a small amount of olive oil. Drain well. Spread cheese mixture over dough and top with onion and cooked lamb. Sprinkle ground cinnamon on top if desired. Bake in a preheated 450° oven for about 7 minutes. Makes 6 or 7.

BREAD QUICHE

This French bread quiche tart is a cross between a breakfast pizza and a Quiche Lorraine made with pastry dough. Serve for brunch or a light lunch with a green salad.

1½ cups all-purpose flour
1 tsp. dry yeast
1 tbs. sugar
1 tsp. salt
2 tbs. butter
½ cup milk, lukewarm

Make yeast dough according to directions, page 6. Allow dough to rise at least 1 hour after the first kneading. Punch down dough briefly and roll on a lightly floured work surface into a 9-inch circle. Line a greased 9-inch round (or tart) pan. Press down center of dough so that a slightly raised border is formed. Prick dough in several places to prevent it from bubbling. Let rise for about 15 to 20 minutes. Sides of dough should rise higher, forming a slight edge. Fill quiche shell and bake in a preheated 350° oven for 25 to 30 minutes or until a toothpick inserted into the center comes out clean. Makes 6 to 8 servings.

BREAD QUICHE

QUICHE FILLING

I use whole milk in this recipe instead of heavy cream to cut the amount of fat. Skim milk is not recommended. I beat the eggs in a blender or food processor with the seasonings, but that is optional. If using Swiss cheese, use white pepper instead of black.

6-8 slices bacon, cooked and crumbled
2-3 green onions, finely chopped
½ cup grated Swiss, cheddar or Gruyère cheese (2 oz.)
2 eggs
¼ cup whole milk, or cream
salt and black or white pepper to taste
freshly grated nutmeg to taste, optional

Sprinkle bacon, onions and cheese into the bottom of a dough-lined tart pan. Beat together eggs, milk and seasonings and pour over all. Fills 1 quiche.

ZATA

This is a Middle Eastern version of Italian focaccia. The thickness of the dough when rolled determines if you have a thin, crispy crust or a thicker, chewier crust. Make the dough into small, pita-sized breads or one large bread. I prefer one large bread which is easily cut into pie-shaped wedges for appetizers or to accompany a meal.

2 cups all-purpose flour
1½ tsp. dry yeast (active or rapid)
½-1 tsp. salt

⅔-¾ cup warm water
1 tbs. olive oil

Make yeast dough following the directions on page 6. Let rise for about 1 hour after kneading. After the rise, or upon completion of the dough cycle if using a bread machine, punch down dough and roll into a 9-inch diameter circle. The dough will be slightly sticky and it is best to not add flour unless absolutely necessary. Place on a greased, perforated pizza pan or a cornmeal-covered pizza peel. For a lighter crust, cover the dough and let it rise for approximately 30 minutes in a warm, draft-free location. Brush the top with olive oil, sprinkle with toppings and bake on a pizza stone if you have one, or bake on pan in a preheated 500° oven for 7 to 10 minutes. Makes 6 to 8 servings.

ZATA

ZAHTAR TOPPING

Zahtar is a Middle Eastern herb blend which may be found in specialty shops or through mail order sources. Dried thyme or oregano make good substitutions.

2-3 tbs. toasted sesame seeds
about 1 tbs. olive oil, or less

1 tbs. dried zahtar
freshly ground pepper to taste

While dough is rising, sauté sesame seeds in a very small amount of olive oil in a large skillet over medium heat, stirring constantly. Be very careful not to burn. Brush oil over top of dough. Spread remaining ingredients evenly over top and bake in a preheated 500° oven for 7 to 10 minutes. Makes about 1/4 cup.

SEEDED ZATA TOPPING

This is a traditional combination of seeds for zata.

1 tbs. sesame oil
1 tsp. cumin
1 tbs. poppy seeds

1/2 tsp. anise seeds
freshly grated Parmesan cheese to taste

Brush sesame oil over top of dough. Spread remaining ingredients evenly over top and bake in a preheated 500° oven for 7 to 10 minutes. Makes about 1/4 cup.

ZATA

HERBED ZATA

This flavored dough goes well with any zata topping, but I especially like it with the pine nut topping that follows. I generally use parsley or basil, but any of your favorite fresh herbs may be used.

2 cups all-purpose flour
1½ tsp. dry yeast (active or rapid)
½-1 tsp. salt
2-4 tbs. chopped fresh herbs

1-2 tsp. minced garlic
⅔-¾ cup warm water
1 tbs. olive oil

Make yeast dough following the directions on page 6. Allow a 1-hour rise. After the rise, or upon completion of the dough cycle, punch down dough and roll into a 9-inch diameter circle. Dough will be slightly sticky and it is best to not add flour unless absolutely necessary. Place on a greased, perforated pizza pan or a cornmeal-covered pizza peel. For a lighter crust, you may cover and let dough rise for approximately 30 minutes in a warm, draft-free location. Brush top with olive oil, sprinkle on toppings and bake on a pizza stone if you have one, or simply bake on a pan as normal in a preheated 500° oven for 7 to 10 minutes. Makes 6 to 8 servings.

ZATA

PINE NUT ZATA

This is based on a Lebanese recipe that makes a great nontraditional topping for zata. Pine nuts may be found in grocery stores or in bulk, which is less expensive, from mail order sources.

½ cup pine nuts (1¾ oz. jar)
2 tbs. olive oil
1 tsp. minced garlic, optional
½ tsp. cayenne pepper, or to taste
½-1 tsp. coarse salt

Process nuts in a food processor or blender until finely chopped. Mix together olive oil, garlic if desired, and cayenne pepper. Spread over dough, leaving a ½-inch border around sides. Spread ground pine nuts on top and sprinkle with salt. Makes enough for 1 zata recipe.

FLATBREADS AS WRAPS

Flatbreads are used throughout the world to wrap meat and cheese fillings, creating an edible holder for the meal. These delicious packets can be found in Europe, the Middle East, Asia, Russia, the Iberian Peninsula and the South American continent. They go by different names (börek, empanadas, kolaches, English pasties, kreplachs, pierogi, potstickers, etc.). They may be eaten hot or cold.

The dough may be a leavened yeast dough or a thin phylo dough, but often is more akin to a pie crust or a flaky pastry dough. Recipes for doughs and fillings seem unlimited. One dough recipe uses cream cheese, another ice water, and yet another eggs and butter. The filled dough may be baked or fried, depending on the recipe.

Any meat, cheese or fruit-filled pastry recipe may be made in very small, bite-sized pastries (2-inch rounds with a heaping teaspoon of filling), medium-sized (3- or 4-inch rounds with ½ to a scant tablespoon of filling) or large, (6- or 8-inch rounds with ¼ to ⅓ cup filling) for a more substantial meal. It is even possible to divide the dough and filling in half and make two large pastries — just bake them a little longer.

TURKISH BÖREK DOUGH

Börek are meat and/or cheese-filled "turnovers" with a bread or pastry wrapper. Larger ones may be eaten as a snack or small meal, while smaller versions may easily be used for appetizers. I highly recommend using butter in this recipe.

3 cups all-purpose flour
½ tsp. salt
1 cup (2 sticks) butter, cold

1 egg
2-4 tbs. ice water

In a large bowl, mix together flour and salt. Work butter into flour by rubbing with your fingers or using a pastry blender. Mix in egg. Slowly add water until dough forms a smooth, soft ball. Place dough in the refrigerator for about 1 hour.

Roll dough on a lightly floured counter as thinly as possible. Cut dough into desired sizes with a biscuit cutter or a glass. Place filling in the center of each circle. Fold one side over, pinching all around to seal into a half-circle shape. Place on an ungreased baking sheet and bake for 30 to 40 minutes in a preheated 350°oven. Yield will depend on size.

TIP: One trick which I use when making pastries like this is to roll the dough as thinly as I can and cut the rounds using a 3-inch biscuit cutter. I then roll each round so that it is slightly larger and hence, thinner and flakier. The added benefit is that this size is perfect for using a dumpling press!

TURKISH BÖREK DOUGH

BÖREK CHEESE FILLING

Use only freshly grated Parmesan cheese for this filling. Pre-grated Parmesan cheese which has been refrigerated will do, although grating it yourself is preferred. Add about 1/4 cup chopped, fresh herbs for extra flavor and color. Choose herbs to complement the meal.

12 oz. grated mozzarella cheese (3 cups)
3 oz. freshly grated Parmesan and/or romano cheese (3/4 cup)
2 eggs
white pepper to taste

Mix cheeses together, blend in egg and season to taste. Fill börek as described on page 130. Makes about 4 cups.

TIP: The lamb filling for pitas (page 97) may also be used for börek.

TURKISH BÖREK DOUGH

GREEK SPINACH FILLING (SPANAKOPETA)

This Greek dish is traditionally served baked in phylo or a pastry dough. I use **Turkish Börek Dough***. The key to this is allowing the spinach to stand with the salt, which pulls out excess moisture. Otherwise, the filling will be soggy. For convenience, I use frozen chopped spinach leaves, thawed. If you prefer fresh spinach, use ½ to 1 cup. The washed, drained leaves should form a ball about the size of an egg.*

1 tsp. salt
1 pkg. (10 oz.) frozen chopped spinach, thawed
2 tbs. finely chopped onion
8 oz. feta cheese, crumbled
2 eggs, beaten
1 tbs. olive oil
pepper to taste

Mix salt with spinach and allow to sit in a colander in the sink for about 15 minutes. Squeeze out any excess moisture. Mix together all remaining ingredients and fill pastries. Brush top of pastries with melted butter. Bake according to directions on page 130. Makes 1 to 1½ cups.

BASIC MEAT PASTRY DOUGH

The secret to this being a flaky, light dough is the ice water. This basic dough is used for empanadas, kolaches, börek or piroshki. The only difference is the name! This recipe is lower in fat, and interchangeable with the **Turkish Borek** *recipe on page 130.*

3 cups all-purpose flour
½ tsp. salt
½ cup (1 stick) butter or margarine,
  cold, cut into cubes

1 egg
about ½ cup ice water

In a large bowl, mix together flour and salt. Using your fingers or a pastry blender, blend in butter until you have the consistency of coarse meal. Blend in egg. Slowly add water, mixing it constantly until dough is just slightly sticky but able to be rolled.

Roll dough on a lightly floured work surface and cut into rounds of desired size using a biscuit cutter, tuna fish can or a similar-sized glass. Place a spoonful of filling in the center and fold pastry over to form a half-moon. Seal by pressing closed with your fingers or the tines of a fork. Bake in a preheated 375° oven for 20 to 25 minutes or until nicely browned. Yield depends on sizes of rounds.

TIP: To make any size pastry desired, see page 129.

BASIC MEAT PASTRY DOUGH

CHILEAN EMPANADAS

*There are few empanadas which stand out like this one. While other ingredients may vary, a **Chilean Empanada** always contains raisins, olives and a hard-boiled egg. If you use a bay leaf, remove it before filling pastries.*

2 tbs. olive oil
1 tsp. paprika
¼ tsp. cayenne pepper, or cumin
½ medium onion, chopped
1 clove garlic, minced
1 lb. ground beef, crumbled
1 tsp. salt

½ tsp. dried oregano, or 1½ tsp.
  chopped fresh
1 bay leaf, or ¼ tsp. bay leaf powder
1 cup beef stock, or beef bouillon
¼ cup raisins
2 tbs. sliced black olives
1 hard-boiled egg, chopped

In a large skillet, heat olive oil, paprika and cayenne. Cook onion and garlic. Add ground beef and seasonings. Cook, stirring occasionally, for about 5 minutes. Add stock and continue cooking, covered, for another 20 minutes or until mixture is not quite dry. Stir occasionally. Remove from heat and mix in raisins and olives. Cool. Once mixture has cooled, stir in eggs and fill pastries. Serve hot or cold. Makes 2 to 2½ cups.

VIENNA PASTRY DOUGH

This pastry dough is often used for meat-filled turnovers or tarts. It can also be rolled and baked into thin crackers.

1/2 cup (1 stick) butter, cold
4 oz. cream cheese, soft
1 cup all-purpose flour
1/2 tsp. salt

Cut butter and cream cheese into several pieces. In a large bowl, mix flour and salt together. Using your fingers or a pastry blender, cut butter into flour until it is the consistency of coarse meal. Continue to blend in cream cheese until a smooth dough is formed. Add a tablespoon or two of flour only if dough is too sticky to work with. Too much flour makes a doughy, heavy pastry. Wrap in plastic or foil and refrigerate for 1 hour or more. Roll dough into a 1/4- to 1/2-inch-thick rectangle and cut rounds of desired size. Fill, fold in half and seal with fingers or the tines of a fork. Bake in a preheated 375° oven for approximately 20 minutes.

VIENNA PASTRY DOUGH

SPANISH CHICKEN EMPANADAS

*The toasted almonds and bacon add a delicious, unique flavor to this filling. This filling may be baked in any of the pastry pie/turnover dough recipes or in **Vienna Pastry Dough**.*

2 tbs. olive oil
1/4 cup chopped almonds
1/2 lb. ground chicken, or ground turkey
2 strips of bacon, finely diced

1/4 medium onion, minced
salt and pepper to taste
1/2 cup grated Swiss cheese, optional

In a large skillet, heat oil and sauté almonds, stirring constantly for a minute or two. Remove from oil and drain on a paper towel. Using the same skillet, cook bacon until it is partially cooked. Pour off excess fat. Add ground meat and onion and cook, stirring, until meat is cooked through. Add nuts and season to taste. Cover and simmer over very low heat for 1 to 2 minutes or until the mixture is warmed. Allow mixture to cool before filling pastry. Sprinkle filling with grated cheese before sealing dough, if desired. Makes about 1 1/2 cups filling, or 2 cups with cheese.

FRIED EMPANADA DOUGH

Fried empanadas cry "appetizers" to me, especially when combined with the following cheese filling.

2 cups all-purpose flour
2 tsp. baking powder
½ tsp. salt
1 tsp. sugar
¼ cup vegetable oil
½ cup water

Combine flour, baking powder, salt and sugar in a large bowl. Make a well in the center and add oil. Mix thoroughly. Add water slowly, mixing until you obtain a consistency which may be easily rolled. Let dough rest for 5 to 10 minutes. Fold dough on a lightly floured work surface and cut into rounds. Spoon filling into the center, and fold dough over to encase it. Seal by pressing tightly with your fingers. Fry in deep fat a minute or so on each side until golden brown. Drain on a paper towel and serve hot or cold. This recipe makes 12 six-inch empanadas or 24 three-inch appetizers.

FRIED EMPANADA DOUGH

SPICY CHEESE

Cheese is a favorite filling for pastries all over the world. This is a variation based on a Spanish recipe. Adjust the hot sauce to taste.

2 cups grated Gruyère cheese
1 egg
½ tsp. hot sauce (Tabasco, Mongolian Fire Oil, etc.)
2-3 tbs. finely chopped walnuts
½ tsp. paprika

Combine cheese and egg. Mix in hot sauce, nuts and paprika. Keep refrigerated if made in advance, but bring up to room temperature prior to filling pastries. Makes a little more than 2 cups.

TURNOVER PASTRY DOUGH, YEAST

While it generally takes longer to make a yeast dough, with a bread machine (or other convenience, such as a heavy-duty mixer) this is actually much easier than some of the preceding pastry doughs and is just as good, and of course lower in fat content. Use this with any meat turnover or pastry meat pie recipe.

3 cups all-purpose flour
1½ tsp. dry yeast (active or rapid)
½ tsp. salt
½ tsp. sugar

1 egg
2 tbs. butter or margarine
¾ cup milk, lukewarm

Make yeast dough according to directions on page 6. Let dough rise for 1½ hours following kneading.

Roll dough on a very lightly floured work surface into a rectangle approximately ¼-inch thick. Cut rounds ranging in size from 3 inches (for appetizers) to 8 or 9 inches (for a meal). Place spoonful(s) of filling in the center of the round. Fold one side over the other, seal by pressing with your fingers or the tines of a fork and brush top with egg white. Place on a greased baking sheet and bake in a preheated 350° oven for 25 to 35 minutes or until golden brown. Yield depends on size of rounds.

TURNOVER PASTRY DOUGH, YEAST

INTERNATIONAL CHICKEN PIES

The use of allspice or cinnamon and nuts in meat-filled pastries is common throughout both the Old and New Worlds. I use ground chicken or turkey, as it seems to blend with the spices, but any ground meat can be used. Use walnuts, pine nuts, hazelnuts or Brazil nuts.

1 clove garlic, minced
1/4 medium onion, finely chopped
1/2 tsp. allspice, or cinnamon
oregano or basil to taste (fresh or dried)
salt and pepper to taste
1/4 cup finely chopped nuts
1 lb. ground chicken or turkey
1 tbs. olive oil, or vegetable oil

Combine all ingredients except oil together in a medium plastic or glass container and refrigerate for 1 or more hours. Cook meat mixture in oil. Allow to cool before filling pastries. Makes a little more than 2 cups.

OREGANO PASTRY DOUGH

The herbs may be chosen to complement any filling used. Try using basil, mint, parsley or cilantro for variations.

3 cups all-purpose flour
1½ tsp. dry yeast (active or rapid)
1 tbs. chopped fresh oregano, or 1 tsp. dried
½ tsp. salt
1 egg
2 tbs. olive oil
¾ cup milk, lukewarm

Make yeast dough according to directions on page 6. Let dough rise for 1½ hours following kneading.

Roll dough on a very lightly floured work surface into a rectangle approximately ¼-inch thick. Cut rounds ranging in size from 3 inches (for appetizers) to 8 or 9 inches (for a meal). Place spoonful(s) of filling in the center of the round. Fold one side over the other, seal by pressing with your fingers or the tines of a fork and brush the top with egg white. Place on a greased baking sheet and bake in a preheated 350° oven for 25 to 35 minutes or until golden brown. Yield depends on size of rounds.

OREGANO PASTRY DOUGH

INTERNATIONAL MEAT PASTRIES

It is difficult to say which nation may take credit for a blend of spices like this. Suffice it to say that it is a blend of the New and Old Worlds. Makes 12 large empanadas for picnic fare.

1-2 cloves minced garlic
¼ medium onion, finely chopped
1 tsp. dried oregano, or 1 tbs. chopped fresh
1 tsp. cumin

salt and pepper to taste
1 lb. ground beef
1 tbs. olive or vegetable oil
½ cup tomato puree or sauce

In a medium glass bowl or plastic container, mix garlic, onion and spices into ground beef. Cook immediately or refrigerate for 1 or more hours. In a large skillet, heat oil and cook meat mixture until crumbled and well done. Add tomato puree or sauce, cover and simmer over low heat, stirring occasionally for 5 to 10 minutes. Remove from heat and allow to cool before filling pastry rounds. Bake as directed. Makes about 2 cups.

BRIOCHE DOUGH

This rich, yeast-leavened French pastry dough is enjoyed as small buns with preserves, or the dough may be used to wrap around meats such as beef or sausage.

2½ cups all-purpose flour
2 tsp. dry yeast
2 tbs. sugar
½ tsp. salt

2 eggs
2 tbs. butter
½ cup milk, lukewarm
beaten egg for sealing dough

Make yeast dough according to directions on page 6. Let dough rise 1 hour after the first kneading. Roll dough on a lightly floured counter into a large rectangle (or 4- to 5-inch rounds). Spread filling in the center, leaving a 1-inch border all around. Lightly brush inside border with a beaten egg. Fold dough into thirds the long way and pinch seams tightly closed with your fingers. Place seam side down on a greased or cornmeal-covered baking sheet (to prevent sticking). Cover and place in a warm, draft-free location and let rise for 30 to 40 minutes. Bake in a preheated 350° oven for 20 to 30 minutes. Let cool and slice into 1- to 1½-inch slices. Makes 12 to 16 slices.

TIP: For fancy appetizers, make rolled pastries using simple ingredients such as thinly sliced cheese (fontina, Gruyère or cheddar) or even jam or preserves.

BRIOCHE DOUGH

BRIE EN BROCHETTE

An herbed Brie makes a delicious appetizer. It literally only takes minutes (especially with a machine to do the kneading), but it looks like you slaved all day!

1 recipe *Brioche Dough*, page 143
1 wheel Brie, about 16 oz.

After dough has risen, roll it into a ½-inch-thick circle on a lightly floured work surface. Remove cheese from box, but leave white (edible) casing on cheese itself. Place cheese in center of dough. Bring border up to encase cheese, trim if necessary and seal tightly. Place on a lightly greased baking sheet, seam side down. Using a sharp knife or razor blade, cut an X on top of brioche. Make a hole in center of X for steam to escape. Cover with a kitchen towel and let rest in a warm, draft-free location for approximately 30 minutes. Lightly brush top with a beaten egg. Bake in a preheated 375° oven for 35 to 40 minutes. Cool on a wire rack. Cut into wedges. Makes about 16 appetizer servings.

CALZONE DOUGH

New York calzones contain only a combination of white cheeses. Elsewhere, calzones may contain white cheeses as well as any number of other filling ingredients. I like to flavor the dough with basil, but you could leave it out if you wish. Calzones may be fried or baked; I prefer baked.

2 cups all-purpose flour
1 tsp. dry yeast (active or rapid)
1 tsp. dried basil, or 1 tbs. chopped fresh
½ tsp. salt
1 tbs. olive oil
⅔ cup water, lukewarm

Make yeast dough according to directions on page 6. After dough has risen about 1 hour, punch it down and divide it into 4 or 5 equal pieces. On a lightly floured work surface, roll each piece into a circle about 7 or 8 inches in diameter.

Place filling in the center of each round and fold half of dough over it so that it is shaped like a half-moon. Using your fingers, pinch seams closed. Place each one on a lightly greased baking pan or pizza sheet. Bake in a preheated 500° oven for approximately 15 minutes. Makes enough for 4 to 5 calzones.

CALZONE DOUGH

WHITE CHEESE BLEND

This combination of cheeses may be used as a filling for calzones or as a topping for any pizza recipe. Add freshly chopped herbs such as basil, oregano, parsley or mint for extra flavor and color. Use only freshly grated Parmesan cheese.

4 oz. ricotta cheese
4 oz. grated mozzarella cheese
1 oz. freshly grated Parmesan cheese

1 tbs. chopped fresh herbs, or to taste, optional

Mix ingredients together, divide evenly into number of calzones being made and place in center of dough rounds. Makes 2 cups.

SAUSAGE CALZONE

I like to use a garlic sausage, or a turkey sausage which is lower in fat.

½ lb. sausage
2 oz. grated provolone cheese (½ cup)

2 oz. grated mozzarella cheese (½ cup)
salt and pepper to taste

In a large skillet, cook sausage until crumbled and cooked through. Drain. Set aside to cool for a brief time. Add remaining ingredients, mix and divide into the number of calzones being made. Makes 2 cups.

STROMBOLI DOUGH

Strombolis may be made from any pizza or calzone dough. It is the method of folding the ingredients inside which makes them unique. The coarsely ground black pepper in this dough brings out the flavor of the filling ingredients.

2 cups all-purpose flour
1 tsp. dry yeast (active or rapid)
½ tsp. salt
1 tsp. coarsely ground black pepper
2 tbs. olive oil
⅔ cup water, lukewarm

Make yeast dough according to directions on page 6. After dough has risen about 1 hour, punch it down and roll on a lightly floured work surface into a large rectangle.

Place filling in the center third of the length of the rectangle. Fold one side over on top of the filling and then the other side on top of that. Using your fingers, pinch the seams closed. Place seam side down on a lightly greased baking pan or pizza sheet. Bake in a preheated 500° oven for approximately 20 minutes. Makes 4 to 5 servings with filling.

STROMBOLI DOUGH

STROMBOLI MEAT FILLING

One of the joys of making strombolis is that you can really use just about any favorite sandwich filling. This combination of cheeses and meats is truly Italian. All ingredient amounts are "guess-timates" — go by what looks right on the dough. Seal tightly.

6 oz. provolone cheese slices
4-6 oz. Italian salami, thinly sliced
4 oz. grated or sliced mozzarella
4-6 oz. Italian ham (proscuitto)

Layer cheeses and meat in the center of the stromboli in the order given. Bake as directed on page 147.

MAIL ORDER SOURCES

Arrowhead Mills, Inc. — 806-364-0730
Box 2059
Hereford, TX 79045

Gray's Grist Mill — 508-636-6075
P. O. Box 422
Adamsville, RI 02801

Kenyon's Corn Meal Co. — 401-783-4054
Usquepaugh, RI 02892

King Arthur's Bakers Catalog — 800-827-6836
Rt. 2, Box 56
Norwich, VT 05055

Tadco/Niblack — 800-724-8883
900 Jefferson Rd. Bldg, 5
Rochester, NY 14623

House of Spices — 718-476-1577
76-17 Broadway
Jackson Heights, NY 11373

Casados Farms — 505-852-2433
P. O. Box 1269
San Juan Pueblo, NM 87566

Colorado Spice Co. — 800-677-7423
5030 Nome Street Unit A
Denver, CO 80239

Pendery's — 800-533-1870
1221 Manufacturing
Dallas, TX 75207

Penzey's Spice House — 414-574-0277
P. O. Box 1448
Waukesha, WI 53187

The Spice House — 414-272-0977
1031 N. Old World 3rd. St.
Milwaukee, WI 53203

Vann's Spices — 410-583-1643
1238 E. Joppa Road
Baltimore, MD 21286

BIBLIOGRAPHY

Bayless, Rick and Bayless, Deann Groen. AUTHENTIC MEXICAN. New York: William Morrow, 1987.

Beard, James. BEARD ON BREAD. New York: Ballantine Books, 1981.

Duff, Gail. BREAD: 150 TRADITIONAL RECIPES FROM AROUND THE WORLD. New York: Macmillan, 1993.

Hultman, Tami, Editor. THE AFRICA NEWS COOKBOOK - AFRICAN COOKING FOR WESTERN KITCHENS. New York: Penquin, 1985.

Hong, Mariana. BREADS OF THE WORLD. New York: Chelsea House, 1977.

Jaffrey, Madhur. INDIAN COOKING. New York: Barron's, 1982.

Jones, Judith and Evan. THE BOOK OF BREAD. New York: Harper and Row, 1982.

Kimball, Yeffe and Anderson, Jean. THE ART OF AMERICAN INDIAN COOKING. New York: Doubleday, 1965.

Mallos, Tess. THE COMPLETE MIDDLE EAST COOKBOOK. Rutland, Vermont: Charles E. Tuttle, 1993.

Ortiz, Elizabeth Labert. THE COMPLETE BOOK OF MEXICAN COOKING. New York: M. Evans, 1967.

Roden, Claudia. A BOOK OF MIDDLE EASTERN FOOD. New York: Vintage Books, 1968.

Salloum, Mary. A TASTE OF LEBANON. New York: Interlink Books, 1988.

Sparks, Pat and Swanson, Barbara. TORTILLAS! New York: St. Martin's Press, 1993.

von Bremzen, Anya and Welchman, John. PLEASE TO THE TABLE. New York: Workman, 1990.

INDEX

SERVE CREATIVE, EASY, NUTRITIOUS MEALS WITH NITTY GRITTY® COOKBOOKS

Cooking with Parchment Paper
The Garlic Cookbook
Flatbreads From Around the World
From Your Ice Cream Maker
Favorite Cookie Recipes, revised
Cappuccino/Espresso: The Book of Beverages
Indoor Grilling
Slow Cooking
The Best Pizza is Made at Home
The Well Dressed Potato
Convection Oven Cookery
The Steamer Cookbook
The Pasta Machine Cookbook
The Versatile Rice Cooker
The Dehydrator Cookbook
The Bread Machine Cookbook
The Bread Machine Cookbook II
The Bread Machine Cookbook III

The Bread Machine Cookbook IV
The Bread Machine Cookbook V
Worldwide Sourdoughs From Your Bread Machine
Recipes for the Pressure Cooker
The New Blender Book
The Sandwich Maker Cookbook
Waffles
The Coffee Book
The Juicer Book
The Juicer Book II
Bread Baking (traditional), revised
The Kid's Cookbook
No Salt, No Sugar, No Fat Cookbook, revised
Cooking for 1 or 2, revised
Quick and Easy Pasta Recipes, revised
15-Minute Meals for 1 or 2

The 9x13 Pan Cookbook
Extra-Special Crockery Pot Recipes
Chocolate Cherry Tortes and Other Lowfat Delights
Low Fat American Favorites
Now That's Italian!
Fabulous Fiber Cookery
Low Salt, Low Sugar, Low Fat Desserts
Healthy Cooking on the Run, revised
Healthy Snacks for Kids
Muffins, Nut Breads and More
The Wok
New Ways to Enjoy Chicken
Favorite Seafood Recipes
New International Fondue Cookbook
Authentic Mexican Cooking

Write or call for our free catalog.
BRISTOL PUBLISHING ENTERPRISES, INC.
P.O. Box 1737, San Leandro, CA 94577
(800) 346-4889; in California (510) 895-4461